# Modern Music Systems

a new perspective on
music scales, clefs,
and chords

Joseph L. D'Agostino

**Modern Music Systems: a new perspective on music scales, clefs, and chords**

In this text, we introduce the following: three new systems (*The Scale Phrase System, System C Clef Notation,* and *System 2000 Chord Notation*), which are the core concepts of this book; ten new terms (*base chord, 5th Chord, common line, brace line, tone lining, solo lining, unison lining, octave lining, parallel lining,* and *alternating lining*); and the new Post-Glarean modes names. Though we have made every attempt to ensure that the information in this book is factual, sensible, and useful, the accuracy and completeness thereof are not guaranteed or warranted.

ISBN-10: 1-44042-866-2
ISBN-13: 978-1-44042-866-1

Joseph L. D'Agostino gives special thanks to Michael Mauldin of Albuquerque, NM, and Linda D'Agostino of Hershey, PA.

Printed in the United States of America

# Contents

Preface     4

1   Three New Systems     5

2   Nomenclature     7

3   *System C Clef Notation*     15

4   Intervals     27

## The Scale Phrase System

5   The Scale Phrase     31

6   Scale Construction     37

7   Scale Descriptions     39

8   Eight-tone Scales     49

9   Other Scales     55

10   The Scale Phrase in Practice     61

## System 2000 Chord Notation

11   The System 2000 Chord Symbol     65

12   Base Chords     73

13   Modified Chords     77

14   Other Chords     85

15   Combinations     93

16   *Tone Lining*     97

Index     99

# PREFACE

Josephine Lowndes Sevely, in *Eve's Secrets*, emphasizes the relevance of "naming": "Furthermore, the naming of a structure is important for a number of obvious reasons. Names help to identify what one is talking about, aid in communication, and in themselves sharpen the awareness of one part as distinct from another."

Providing further insight into the process of critical organization, Will Durant, in *The Story of Philosophy*, informs us: "Without these Ideas—these generalizations, regularities and ideals—the world would be to us as it must seem to the first-opened eyes of a child, a mass of unclassified and unmeaning particulars of sensation; for meaning can be given to things only by classifying and generalizing them, by finding the laws of their beings, and the purposes and goals of their activity."

And, finally, the great Confucius is credited with these words: "He who by reanimating the Old can gain knowledge of the New is fit to be a teacher."

In the spirit of those cited above, we humbly offer a new perspective. We believe that traditional or classical systems or concepts, though they may be long outdated, are certainly not irrelevant; they profoundly influence and contribute to the new method. The new method, however, is ordinarily not simply new: it is inevitable. That premise was the primary impetus for us in introducing these new systems.

For several decades, we investigated Western music literature in an effort to see if everything that *could* be said in Western music theory *had* been said. Was every potentially useful idea considered? And, if so, was each respective idea fully developed? Was every possible method considered and consequently employed? Ultimately, we found that there were four areas in which improvement might justifiably be made, even if only from a theoretical point of view.

In developing these new perspectives, we kept in mind the duty of providing the reader with genuinely new and truly useful ideas. Simply iterating existing, centuries-old theories and then sugarcoating them would not be enough. Our goal was to provide the absolutely best method for learning eight-tone scales and chords, so much so that musicians could safely and confidently abandon the old methods, once and for all. Additionally, we offer a new clef system, one which is just about as simple and straightforward as any clef system could be; and we offer new terminology for lines of tones written for orchestra.

We thank you kindly for considering *Modern Music Systems: a new perspective on music scales, clefs, and chords*. We have done our best to present our ideas as clearly and succinctly as possible. We believe that once you've grasped these new concepts and then exercised them, you will realize their beauty. We hope you will embrace these three new systems and recommend them to others. We learned very many things while creating this book, and we had very much fun. We wish the same for you.

*Joseph L. D'Agostino*

# Chapter 1

# THREE NEW SYSTEMS

If there is one thing that the history of music tells us, it is that it seemingly takes forever for any major, meaningful changes to take place in music theory. Even now, there are literally thousands of music publications on the market, covering virtually ever musical topic that can be imagined. And yet, regarding theory, the forward pace is, at best, a snail's pace. Could it be that there is little left to theorize? Nothing worthy to investigate? Have inquiring minds "run the gamut"?

Music is often thought of as the universal language. That may be the case from the perspective of *listening* to the music, but it is certainly not the case from the perspective of *notating* and *interpreting* the music for performance. Until now, we haven't had a system that has provided clear communication between composers, performers, and the like. Sometimes, to bridge gaps of communication, a blending of two schools of thought is employed. That blending may prove useful at first, but as the blending is allowed to continue, and as new concepts are assimilated into the mix, confusion usually results. This appears to be the case at present. If you consider how long Jazz and Popular music have been around, you would think that by now someone would have developed a standardized, simplified, and universally accepted system of chord notation, octave identification, and scale identification and classification. So, has the gamut *truly* been run?

We think not. Moreover, we think that today would be an opportune time to introduce our three new systems— *The Scale Phrase System*, *System C Clef Notation*, and *System 2000 Chord Notation*. These three systems showcase the manifestation of form inevitable in practical music theory. Each system is a response to the directive of musical evolutionary process, and each is a response that won't disappoint the modern musician. These new, complementary systems are each designed to perform two specific functions: to simplify and to standardize. To accomplish these tasks, we stress accuracy in naming and notation. We strive to be as accurate as possible, not only to establish a sound theoretical base from which to work but to make communication between musicians as clear as possible. To reinforce and validate the three new concepts introduced in this text, traditional theory is minimally covered and discussed. To keep these new systems as simple and concise as possible, very few new symbols or terms are introduced, and when new symbols or terms are introduced, their inclusion serves only to more accurately reflect structure and order.

*The Scale Phrase System*

The subject of scales and modes can be confusing, especially for the new student. One of the principal reasons for this is that the present method of scale construction, identification, and classification is actually a mixed bag of methods, one which condones the coalescence of two schools of thought—one traditional and one contemporary. We have scale names such as Lydian Dominant, Lydian Augmented, Major Locrian, and Half-diminished. In the name Lydian Dominant, for example, the word Lydian implies modal (mode) qualities, and the word Dominant implies tonal (scale) qualities, as well as function. These sorts of implications may be understood and embraced by the learned musician, but for those struggling to make sense of music nomenclature, some of which has been used for centuries, these implications can cause confusion and make the process of memorization difficult.

The Scale Phrase System (SPS) presents eight-tone scales as structures logically formed of distinctive constituents—*scale phrases*. Most of the scales demonstrated in this book are even named directly from the scale phrases used to build them. The SPS demonstrates features, intervals, and groupings that are characteristic of each of those scales, providing the student with the theoretical tools to confidently construct, determine, and analyze SPS eight-tone scales, which are actually existing contemporary scales seen from a different perspective. To benefit from this system, all the new student needs is the desire to learn and the willingness to make a little effort; all the trained musician needs is an open mind.

*System C Clef Notation*
System C Clef Notation is the simplest, most concise, and easiest-to-use clef notation system yet developed. System C resuscitates the dying C clef, and politely informs the G and F clefs that they have overstayed their welcome. Employing only *one* clef type, System C is easily learned by the new student and easily adopted by the trained musician. After seeing how System C compares to the contemporary clef system, the novice or professional musician will quickly realize this new system's superiority in pitch and octave identification.

*System 2000 Chord Notation*
For the longest time, the consensus on chord symbol notation has not been one of unanimity. In 1976, Carl Brandt and Clinton Roemer offered *Standardized Chord Symbol Notation: a Uniform System for the Music Profession.* Though it was the only serious, in-depth work on chord symbol notation to that point in the century, and though it made some theoretically sound points, it didn't resolve the debate over which was the correct way to symbolize chords, a debate which apparently continues to this day. However, we strongly feel that the debate simply does not need to continue. We feel that System 2000 brings the long awaited "accord" over chord symbol notation.

System 2000 is a simple, straightforward system of chord notation that provides the student with the incentive to state the properties of a chord as they literally exist. System 2000 is designed to make communication between musicians remarkably clear, leaving little room for misunderstanding or misinterpretation. Using System 2000, it is virtually impossible to misinterpret the elements of any given chord. The chord, to be a powerful, effectual structure, must be exact and concise. To achieve that end, System 2000 provides the means. The chord should inherently give an estimation of vertical quality and mood, and it should suggest complementary tones. But the chord can not do that if it is not exact. As notated with System 2000, every chord is exact. We guarantee it.

**Modern Music Systems: a new perspective on music scales, clefs, and chords**
As you make your way through this text, you will hear our watchwords—"to simplify and to standardize." The goal of simplifying and standardizing is indeed a good goal, but it is not good enough. To do better than that, we offer something genuinely new. And when we say "new," we mean just that; you will not find hackneyed traditional music theory simply repackaged with better graphics and brighter colors. We simply wish to offer some new ideas wrapped in a package that is unassuming, yet one fine enough to make the point and withstand repeated use.

We have attempted to provide material that is beneficial to musicians, regardless of their respective levels, and we have striven to provide a text that is easy to read, one laid out simply and logically. For optimum benefit, we encourage the self-teaching student to employ three practices: (1) Looking up any unfamiliar terms or concepts. We hope that the scope of the student's studies will extend well beyond the confines of this book; (2) Being patient with the text. The text that follows the initiatory text (even if it comes one or more chapters later) often clarifies or validates the initiatory text; and (3) Taking one step at a time. These new concepts are not difficult ones, and the student will realize this fact if he or she takes whatever amount of time is needed to grasp the material.

New students who are receiving professional instruction will be introduced to three simple and concise systems. The inclusion of these new systems at the onset of new students' musical training will help avoid confusion later in their respective courses of study; and as the theory used to support our new concepts is fundamentally minimal, the instructor may choose to elaborate on any particular topic covered in this text.

Trained musicians, on the intermediate or professional level, will most likely already have a fair knowledge of theory. As such, they should easily be able to assimilate these new systems into their respective musical repertoires.

# Chapter 2

# NOMENCLATURE

Learning the systems introduced in this book will be made much easier if we have a clear understanding of the terms used. If we clarify any terms that may later cause confusion, we should be able to breeze through the minimal theory involved in presenting these new systems. Over the years, some musical terms have been introduced, and some have been dropped. Some terms (e.g., *tone* and *note*) have become somewhat synonymous. Regardless whether the terms are old or new, we must have a clear understanding of what they are intended to mean as used in these new systems. Let's now discuss and clarify those terms so that we may keep communication clear and make the learning process easy.

## Tone and Note

These two little words—spelled in fact using the same letters—have caused and can cause confusion to students new to music, so we will clarify the two terms. Clarification will be made simplest by first defining the word *note*.

Note: a written symbol representing a single sound of a given musical pitch and duration.

An example of "a written symbol" is an "eighth note," shown here placed on a five-line stave.

"A single sound of a given musical pitch" is a *tone*. We can not show an example symbol for a tone, for a tone is *heard*, not seen.

"Pitch" is the standardized association of a particular frequency and a pitch name. For example, A4 would be 440 Hertz (Hz), or cycles per second. (We will discuss pitch and tone names in Chapters 3 and 4.)

So, what all that basically mean is this: If you were to look at a given page of music, a written *note* would prompt you to produce the *tone* represented by that written *note*. If you then depress the piano *key* that corresponds to that written *note* (let's say A4), the action of that depression would cause the sounding a *tone*, and that *tone,* in most cases, would be at a specific (generally standardized) *pitch*.

Now, all of this may seem to be a roundabout way of clarifying two minor terms, but it is nonetheless important, for the term *tone* will be used predominantly in this text. We can hear a tone, but we can not, technically, hear a note. We can *write* a note on a music stave, but when we play the instrument to produce the actual sound, the sound heard is a *tone*.

As the two terms relate to scales and modes, we must mention one very important point: the eight-*tone* scale (featured in this book) will have eight *different* tones, which means that each tone's pitch will be different from that of the others. An eight-*note* scale—for whatever unusual purpose—could conceivably have two or more of the *same* exact notes, or it could have two enharmonic notes (i.e., *different* notes representing tones of the same pitch).

Additionally, to prevent confusion when we later discuss the SPS scale names and the contemporary scale names, we must point out something important: In contemporary music theory, the word *tone* is sometimes used to mean "an interval equivalent to a '*major 2nd*' (2 half steps)." In this book, we will *not* use the term *tone* in that context. In the SPS, our *major 2nd* interval is indeed two half steps, but we refer to it as one "whole step," not one "whole tone." We do so in an effort to keep the term *tone* to mean just that—a single *sound* at a given pitch—and not to suggest distance or intervals. The contemporary term "semi-tone," for example, is peculiar. Though it is intended to mean "one half step," it semantically suggests "one-half of a tone," which, from a physics standpoint, can only sensibly suggest some form of duration. Without elaborating any further, we iterate that we have carefully chosen to predominantly use the term *tone* in this book.

## Interval

By strict definition, the *interval* is the "relationship" or "difference in pitch" between tones. You may also hear the term "interval" referred to as the "distance" between two tones. You may look at a piano keyboard and think of distance, for example, the distance between the C4 key and the D4 key. If you played a C4, then two hours later played a D4, you would (if you weren't asleep by then) most likely feel "distance"—an extraordinary distance! However, if in an ordinary, sensible fashion, you played a C4 followed immediately by a D4, you would likely hear or feel a "difference," a difference in pitch between the two tones. Ordinarily, you would perceive a "difference" rather than a "distance." However, as the interval relates to the message in this book, you may rudimentarily think of the interval as a "distance," if you so choose, and not feel that you are thinking incorrectly about it.

## Half Step

A *half step* is the smallest interval in modern music. On the piano, it is the distance between two immediately adjacent keys, whether black or white. An example would be the distance between E4 and F4 (see figure 2.1).

In nearly all modern music, the half step is determined by a system called *Equal Temperament*. In the Equal Temperament (ET) system, the octave is divided into twelve equal half steps. Though there are other ways of creating specific intervals (with different systems of tempering), the twelve half steps devised using the ET system are the half steps that we refer to in this book.

To better visualize this, figure 2.1 shows the layout of some of the keys of the piano. Any two immediately adjacent keys are one half step apart.

figure 2.1

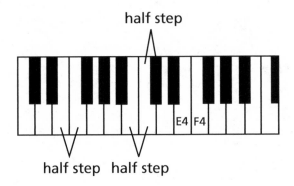

Figure 2.2 shows a section of frets on the neck of the guitar. Any two immediately adjacent frets are one half step apart.

figure 2.2

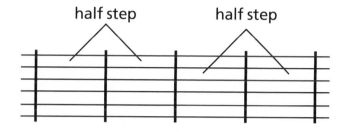

As you will soon discover, the half step is the foundation of the SPS.

## Stave and Clef

Music notation in this text is done employing an elongated symbol called the *stave*. Each stave comprises five lines and the four spaces between them. These lines and spaces are called *staff degrees*. Figure 2.3 shows a single stave.

figure 2.3

The stave, though it is the backbone of music notation, is of little value without the *clef* symbol. The clef symbol, notated on the stave at the beginning of a line of music, denotes that the tones represented on that particular stave fall within a specified, established range of pitch. Figure 2.4 shows a stave with a clef symbol. This particular clef symbol is the "C5," one of the clef symbols employed in *System C Clef Notation*, the clef system used throughout this text. (We will formally introduce and demonstrate System C in Chapter 3.)

figure 2.4

Whenever a tone is represented on a staff degree (a line or a space), its *letter name* is automatically determined. For example, a note symbol placed on the first (bottom) line of the stave in figure 2.4 represents the tone E. Any note symbol placed on that line will represent some sort of E. Even if the note symbol is modified with an *accidental* (e.g., a *sharp* [♯] or a *flat* [♭] ) it will still be some form of E. The accidental called a *natural* (♮) cancels any sharp or flat, thereby returning the tone to its natural pitch.

## Scale

A *scale* is a unified collection of successive pitches (a sequence of tones) arranged in order of lowest to highest or highest to lowest. The scale starts on a fundamental tone, normally referred to as the *tonic* or *key tone*. Ordinarily, a scale will provide a sense of being a structure that is complete in itself.

## Eight-tone Scale

In most contemporary texts, the scale that the SPS refers to as the *eight-tone scale* will be denoted as a scale with only *seven* pitches (i.e., the tonic and six subsequent scale tones, with the octave of the tonic *not* being considered a constituent). In the SPS, however, the octave of the tonic is considered as an integral part of the scale, and not simply because of the manner in which the SPS constructs scales. The word *scale* comes from the Latin word *scala*, which means "ladder." A ladder is most useful for getting from one vertical point to another. Imagine, however, if the top rung of the ladder were permanently missing. The ladder would likely still be useful, but the sense of being "complete in itself" (as noted in the definition of a scale) would be diminished.

In the first section of this book, one of the topics that we focus on is that of the *eight-tone scale*. As built and employed in the SPS, our eight-tone scale is a scale with a total of *eight* different, successive tones. The eight tones include the tonic (the fundamental tone), six scale tones, and the octave of the tonic (a repeat of the tonic twelve half steps higher than the tonic). Figure 2.5 shows an example of an eight-tone scale; this particular scale is the C Major Scale, a scale which will be discussed later.

figure 2.5

In the SPS, the eight-tone scale has, from the first tone to the last tone, a total of *twelve* half steps—no more, no less. The interval between tones can be that of one half step, two half steps (one whole step), or three half steps. The eight-tone scale may *not* include an interval that has more than three half steps. As you will discover later, our SPS eight-tone scale is built with two *scale phrases* conjoined by a *bridge step*. (We will demonstrate and explain the scale phrase in Chapter 5, and the bridge step in Chapter 6.)

## Scale Degrees

When we talk about the individual tones of any eight-tone scale, we refer to those individual tones as *scale degrees*. Each of those scale degrees has a specific name. Figure 2.6 shows an example scale, the C Major Scale, and its scale degrees' names.

figure 2.6

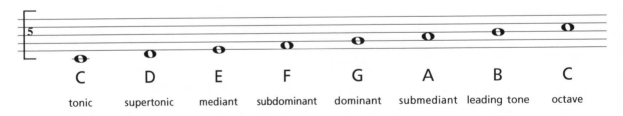

The scale shown above starts with the tone C, called the *tonic* or *key tone*. If, for example, a scale starts with the C as the tonic, that scale is referred to as being "in the key of C." The tonic is the fundamental tone, the tone upon which the whole scale is based; as such, it is the most important tone in the scale. The tonic will ordinarily be found to be (or be perceived to be) a point of departure and an ending point, while the other tones of the scale will function in relation to the tonic. At some point in your studies, you will discover that given scales and given chords (discussed later) will have a distinct relationship to a given key.

In the above scale, we see that the fifth tone, the G, is called the *dominant*. In this particular scale, the G tone is more specifically referred to as "the dominant of C" because the scale is in the key of C. The dominant has traditionally been viewed as a strong scale degree because the Dominant *chord*, the chord built on the dominant scale degree, is a very important chord. (We discuss chords in the *System 2000 Chord Notation* section of this book, with a detailed discussion of the Dominant chord in Chapter 11.) The leading tone is another strong scale degree; when the leading tone is employed in a melodic line, it has a tendency to "lead up to" the tonic. In figure 2.6, if the seventh scale degree were one half step lower (i.e., a B♭ instead of a B), that scale degree could be referred to as the *subtonic*.

## Mode

A *mode* is a unified collection of successive pitches (a sequence of tones) arranged in order of lowest to highest or highest to lowest. The mode starts on a fundamental tone, normally referred to as the *final*. In this chapter, we emphasize the process of mode formation because in later chapters, many of the scales demonstrated are essentially modes of other scales.

Historically, the modes existed long before any scales did. To educate the student on the modes, an instructor may cover the detailed, complex, and lengthy history of the origination and development of the modes, and then proceed into the discussion of scales. That's the chronological way. There is, however, another way which is quicker and easier, and that is to more or less work backwards. With figures 2.7 and 2.8, we will demonstrate the quicker and easier way.

Figure 2.7 displays the tones of the C Major Scale, a common scale that has no sharps or flats in it.

figure 2.7

We see from figure 2.7 that the tones included are C, D, E, F, G, A, B, and C. If we try to build a scale using *only* those select tones, but start (and end) the scale on D instead of C, we will have formed a mode. Figure 2.8 shows the resulting mode.

figure 2.8

As you can see, this is a mode built on (or from) a scale. Though historically this may seem backwards, it is an effective and quick way to show how to form a mode. The mode in figure 2.8 is the Dorian mode—the Dorian of C. It is *not* the Dorian of D; this mode is the Dorian of C because the mode is built on the specific tones of the C Major Scale.

Now we'll show all of the seven modes that can be built on the tones of the C Major Scale. The modes shown on page 12 are given in the *modern* order, not the order in which they originated historically; and they are given with their established names. Each of the modes is a mode "of C" (i.e., the Ionian of C, the Dorian of C, the Phrygian of C, and so forth).

## Ionian of C

This mode is built by starting on the tone C. As you can see, this is also the C Major Scale.

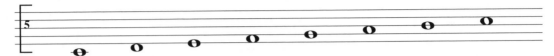

## Dorian of C

This mode starts on the tone D. Remember: We are using *only* the tones of the C Major Scale.

## Phrygian of C

This mode starts on the tone E.

## Lydian of C

This mode starts on the tone F.

## Mixolydian of C

This mode starts on the tone G.

## Aeolian of C

This mode starts on the tone A.

## Locrian of C

This mode starts on the tone B.

As you become more familiar with scales and modes, you will discover that the seven modes built on the tones of the Major Scale use mode signatures that are identical to certain key signatures. For example, on page 49, you will see the eight-tone scales named Major, Minor, Minor 2, Augmented, Major Minor, Minor 3, and Locrian. Each of those scales is intentionally presented in the key of C. As such, each scale has the tone C as its root tone; and the key signature for each scale is one of *no* sharps or flats. (Essentially, those scales have no visible key signatures.)

However, when those very same sequences of tones are employed as modes, they would most likely be used with their appropriate mode signatures. The mode signatures for the above modes—respectively ordered Ionian to Locrian—would be the same as the key signatures for the major keys C, Bb, Ab, G, F, Eb, and Db; and the names of those modes would be Ionian of C, Dorian of Bb, Phrygian of Ab, Lydian of G, Mixolydian of F, Aeolian of Eb, and Locrian of Db. The following chart should help you visualize this particular scale-mode relationship.

| This scale . . . | . . . sounds the same as this mode . . . |
|---|---|
| C Major | Ionian of C |
| C Minor | Dorian of Bb |
| C Minor 2 | Phrygian of Ab |
| C Augmented | Lydian of G |
| C Major Minor | Mixolydian of F |
| C Minor 3 | Aeolian of Eb |
| C Locrian | Locrian of Db |

As far as nomenclature is concerned, we can not overemphasize the benefit of learning good habits in the use of terms and order. We hope the new student will get the message and make every effort to learn good habits right from the start, for bad habits ordinarily are easy to learn but hard to unlearn.

## Tonality

*Tonality* is the relatedness of a group of tones to a central (fundamental) tone called the tonic. By definition, we see that tonality is *dependent* on pitch. For example, a scale "in the key of C" must be built with a tonic of C, which could be C4 (261.6 Hz), C5 (523.2 Hz), or any other C. In our present-day musical system, we have fifteen *major* keys (Cb, C, C#, Db, D, Eb, E, F, F#, Gb, G, Ab, A, Bb, and B) and fifteen *minor* keys (C, C#, D, D#, Eb, E, F, F#, G, G#, Ab, A, A#, Bb, and B). Each of the major keys has its respective *relative minor* key (i.e., one of the minor keys listed above), a key whose tonic is positioned an interval of a *minor third* below the tonic of the major key. (Intervals are discussed in Chapter 4.)

### Key signatures

Once the tonic is confirmed, the key of a given composition (or part of a composition) can be determined by the *key signature*, an ordered group of accidentals placed at the beginning of each stave, directly after the clef symbol. The key signature remains in effect until a new signature is indicated. Figure 2.9 shows three key signatures. You will notice that a given major key and its relative minor key employ the same key signature.

figure 2.9

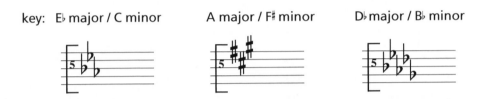

key:  Eb major / C minor        A major / F# minor        Db major / Bb minor

## Modality

*Modality* is the quality of tones arranged in characteristic intervals, those intervals determined by which scale degree of the scale the mode is built on, the quality of that scale degree being determined by which specific scale is used. So, we see here, by definition, that modality is *not* dependent on pitch. Therefore, we essentially can have modes in a far greater number than we can have keys. We can have seven modes built on the scale degrees of the Major Scale, in any of the fifteen keys. We can have seven modes built on the scale degrees of the Minor Scale, in any of the fifteen keys. We can, for that matter, have modes built on the scale degrees of virtually any scale. In this book, we will put considerable emphasis on the seven modes built on the Major Scale and the seven modes built on the Minor Major Scale.

### Mode signatures

Since the design and use of *modes signatures* is noticeably arbitrary, no uniform practice is presently observed in the use of mode signatures. In compositions (or parts of compositions) in which modes are used, mode signatures can prove to be economically useful, providing a means of notation free of the inordinate use of accidentals. Unlike traditional key signatures, mode signatures may incorporate both sharps *and* flats in a single signature, thereby providing concise notation of compositions written predominantly in a given mode, or, in extreme cases, compositions employing two modes simultaneously. Of the huge number of possible mode signatures, three are shown in figure 2.10.

figure 2.10

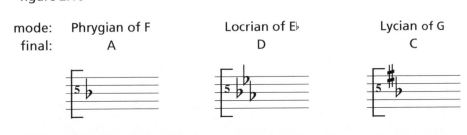

mode:    Phrygian of F        Locrian of Eb        Lycian of G
final:          A                    D                  C

# Chapter 3

# SYSTEM C CLEF NOTATION

*System C Clef Notation* is used throughout this text. It is the simplest, most concise, and easiest-to-use clef notation system yet developed. Employing only *one* clef type, System C is easily learned by the new student and easily adopted by the trained musician. After seeing how System C compares to the traditional and contemporary clef systems, you will quickly realize the system's superiority in pitch and octave identification.

## Forerunners

Before we introduce System C, we will demonstrate the traditional and contemporary clefs. Figure 3.1 shows the traditional clef symbols, which include one G clef, five C clefs, and two F clefs.

figure 3.1

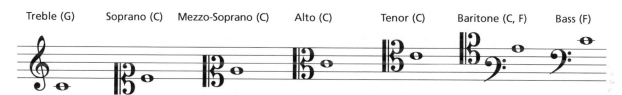

Figure 3.2 shows the contemporary clefs symbols, which are actually a combination of traditional and contemporary clefs. All of the contemporary clefs occupy a fixed position on their respective staves, except the C clef (middle symbol), which, depending on its position on the stave, will function as either the C alto clef or the C tenor clef. Using any of the four contemporary G clefs, the tone G (regardless of the octave) is represented on the second line of any given stave, and using any of the four contemporary F clefs, the tone F (regardless of the octave) is represented on the fourth line of any given stave.

figure 3.2

In figure 3.1, all of the notes shown on the stave are what are referred to as "Middle C" or C4 (261.6 Hz). Different clef symbols are used in music notation so that each respective instrument's part can be written in, or at least very close to, that instrument's useful pitch range.

For those not already familiar with C4 and its position in the pitch spectrum, we will now designate all of the common C tones using the octave designation system of the Acoustical Society of America. In figure 3.3, we have joined two staves, the top one notated with the traditional G (treble) clef, and the bottom one notated with the traditional F (bass) clef. Together, when joined by the traditional *brace* ( { ), that combination of staves may be referred to as a *staff*, or *staff system*. Above and below each individual stave, notes can be written on *ledger lines*. Ledger lines are used for the placement of notes that extend beyond the limit of the staves. Figure 3.3 clearly shows the position of C4 in relation to the other tones in the pitch spectrum. Middle C in figure 3.3 is written on a ledger line.

figure 3.3

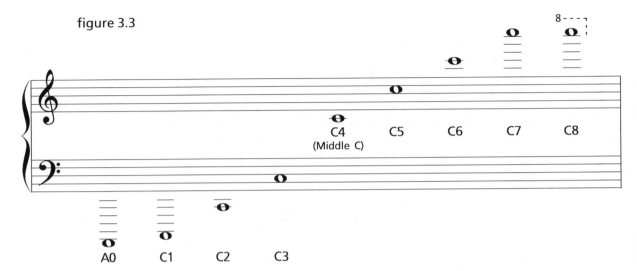

The staff system that you see in figure 3.3—the combination of two staves joined by a brace—is the one that you've been used to seeing in all of the notated music of the past several hundred years, except for that written for instruments that use only one stave, and that written by the avant-garde; and it's likely that you'll be seeing that staff system for an undetermined number of years. You will, however, be seeing it only until System C takes over and becomes the clef system of choice. It will happen, but it may take a few years. Don't be discouraged, though, for the introduction and promotion of System C is timely and appropriate. To validate that claim, we need to take a brief look at the traditional C clef from a historical standpoint and then examine the prospects for that traditional clef.

## Traditional C Clef

At some point in the tenth century, musicians started using a single red line to designate that any *neume* (the predecessor of the "note") placed on that line would represent the tone F (our present-day F3). Shortly after the debut of that innovation, someone began the practice of placing a letter F directly before that line. As such, the F became the first clef symbol in music notation. Later in that century, the original C clef made its debut as the second clef symbol. A letter C was placed directly before a second pitch line (colored yellow or green), a line which was positioned *above* the red F line. The placement of the letter C informed the performer that any tone represented on that line would be a C (our present-day C4). The original C clef's shape was changed a few times over a period of several hundred years, but the clef was still in use until about the mid 1700s. By then, the five-line stave had become generally accepted as standard, and the G clef and the F (bass) clef were relegated to fixed positions. Ultimately, the C clef evolved to its present form, but unlike the G and F clefs, it became movable (see figure 3.1).

Despite its historical significance, recognizable form, and serviceability during certain periods of Classical music (namely the Baroque), the C clef has never become totally embraced; its role has never been secured. There has been for several hundred years—and still remains—a movement toward elimination of the traditional C clefs. Three traditional C clefs are already virtually obsolete: the soprano, the mezzo-soprano, and the baritone. That leaves only the alto and tenor clefs. The only application in which the alto clef is used regularly is that of writing viola parts; it isn't even used for alto voice parts. The tenor clef is presently used only occasionally for high parts written for bassoon, tenor trombone, cello, and bass. Tenor voice parts are written using the G clef, not the tenor clef. Inconspicuous as it may be, the impetus to drive out the C clefs is there. By going with the quiet evolutionary process, musicians, whether professional or novice, are subscribing to the two-clef system, essentially saying that the formerly traditional but now contemporary G and F clefs are adequate, even though use of those clefs is not without limitations. So, as neither of the two remaining C clefs are used much anymore, and as two clefs are easier to learn than four, it is reasonably safe to say that the two remaining traditional C clefs will eventually be cast by the wayside.

But what is necessitated if the old C clefs are indeed eliminated? The contemporary G and F clefs will have to cover for the then obsolete Cs. Contemporary notation already employs modified G and F clefs, so covering for the ousted C should not be an insurmountable task. Yet, often it happens that certain old standbys no longer prove to be adequate. We believe that we are at that point with the contemporary clefs. Having been modified so many times, they are awkward, and having been exposed so long, stale. As such, it would behoove all of us to now make the change to truly modern music notation by first embracing the efficient and economical System C.

Granted, it *is* time to do away with the seemingly awkward traditional C clef; however, it is certainly *not* the time to eradicate the concept of the C clef itself. In truly modern music, the tone C is a familiar and visible tone, and academically, especially for new students, a pivotal tone.* In a most timely manner, the C clef is now reborn in System C in a new, more practical, and more serviceable form. Its role is finally secured. This new clef is not just superior to the traditional C clef, it is superior to *all* existing clefs. It provides the tools for highly efficient octave identification. Let's now take a look at the System C clef.

## System C Clef

Figure 3.4 (middle) shows the System C C5 clef. The System C clef symbol comprises two components: the *clef indicator* (the letter C) and the *pitch indicator* (a number).

figure 3.4

clef indicator        C5 clef on five-line stave        pitch indicator

The *clef indicator*—a tall, narrow, squared-off C—identifies itself as a true C clef. The clef indicator denotes that any note written in the pitch indicator space will represent the tone C.

The *pitch indicator* shows unequivocally which specific tone is represented in that space. In figure 3.4, the number 5 clearly shows that any note written in that space represents the tone C5. The pitch indicator may be written in the *second* or *third* space. The choice of which space the pitch indicator will occupy may depend on the pitch range of the music to be played; the serviceability of that particular clef for the individual performer (i.e., some performers will prefer one clef over another); or any other reason the performer or composer chooses.

The clef indicator's shape and position over the stave are unique: The top arm of the C (extending out to the right) lies precisely at the level at which the first ledger line above the stave would be notated; the bottom arm lies at the level at which the first ledger line below the stave would be notated. As such, the clef indicator and the pitch indicator combination clearly indicate the location of *two* Cs, not just one. For example, the clef symbol in figure 3.4 tells us that the tone represented in the third space is that of C5, and the tone represented on the fourth line below that space is that of C4.

* The lowest C tone (though inaudible) has a frequency of approximately 8 Hz. Interestingly, the human body, in the deeply relaxed "alpha" state, vibrates at a fundamental frequency of 7.83 Hz. This frequency, ordinarily referred to as the Schumann Resonance, is the prominent frequency of the magnetic resonance of the earth's ionospheric cavity, and it is the frequency to which the earth and virtually all life forms are attuned.

Figure 3.5 shows System C clefs and their contemporary counterparts.

figure 3.5

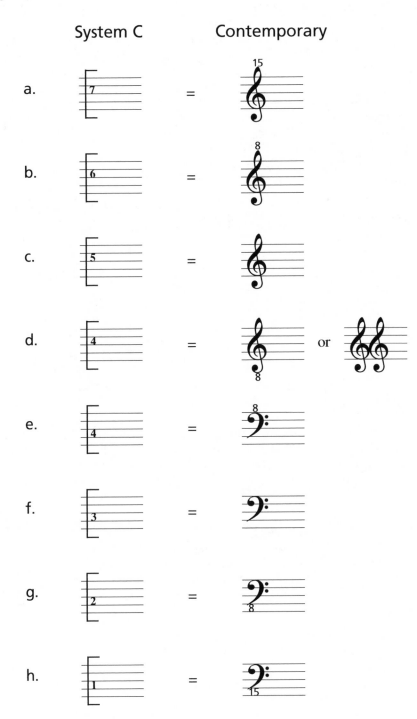

Figure 3.5 shows only eight System C clefs: C7 (high), C6 (high), C5 (high), C4 (high), C4 (low), C3 (low), C2 (low), and C1 (low). Any System C clef (from a C1 to a C8) can be a *high* or a *low*, though it is likely that some of the System C clefs will be used seldom, and some not at all. All of the sixteen System C clefs are shown on page 25.

Some contemporary musicians sometimes employ two other clefs that are not shown in figure 3.5: the "descant" clef, which is equivalent to the System C C7 (high) clef; and the "contrabass" clef, which is equivalent to the System C C1 (low) clef. The shapes of those two contemporary clefs are very similar to the System C contemporary counterparts shown on page 15.

Figure 3.6 shows the staff system of figure 3.3 using System C clefs instead of the contemporary clefs. This system, employing a C5 clef and a C3 (low) clef, can be used for the notation of a piano part.

figure 3.6

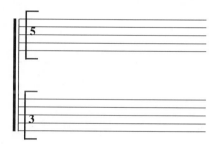

Figure 3.7 shows another staff system, this one employing a C6 clef and a C4 (low) clef. This system can be used for the notation of a celesta part.

figure 3.7

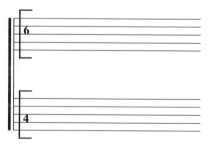

Figure 3.8 shows yet another staff system, this one employing a C4 clef and a C2 (low) clef. This system can be used for the notation of a low part for piano or a low part for harp.

figure 3.8

## System Identifiers

The System C clefs work beautifully with the System C *system identifiers*. Together they provide for neatness and conciseness that is unmatched in contemporary music notation. Figure 3.9 demonstrates the three system identifiers used in System C: the *common line* (A), the *bracket* (B), and the *brace line* (C).

figure 3.9

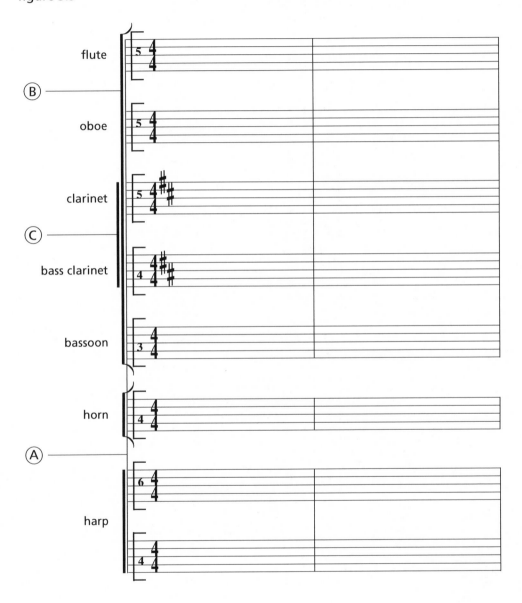

The *common line* is a single thin vertical line which denotes that all of the staves connected by that line are to be read simultaneously. The common line is placed to the left of the clef symbol(s), at the left edge of the lines of the staff (i.e., a single stave or a combination of staves). Ordinarily, on the first page of an orchestral or ensemble score, the common line will denote a full system, the largest of the three possible types of systems in any given work.

The *bracket* comprises the bracket line (a thick line) and two terminal jogs. The bracket denotes that all of the staves contained within that bracket are those of music for instruments all of the same *choir*. An orchestral score may include any or all of the five choirs (woodwind, brass, percussion, chorus, string). The large bracket in figure 3.9 denotes a choir—a woodwind choir. Though the bracket may be used to denote a full system (e.g., in a string quartet score, which involves only one choir), it ordinarily identifies a system of small to moderate size. The bracket will sometimes denote a system of the smallest form, that being one single stave assigned to one or more of the *same* instrument (e.g., small bracket in figure 3.9). The bracket line is placed to the left of the common line.

The *brace, or brace line* (a thick line), is placed to the left of the common line if no bracket is used, or to the left of the bracket line if the bracket is used. The brace line connects the staves of music notated for the following: instruments of the same *family* (e.g., clarinet and bass clarinet in figure 3.9); like instruments or a group of like instruments that have unlike parts; keyboard instruments (examples in figures 3.6 and 3.7); and other instruments that ordinarily require the use of two staves (e.g., harp in figure 3.9). In System C, the brace line—a simple, no-frills line—is used in the same way that the standard brace symbol is used in contemporary music notation (see figure 3.3). Note: Some instruments, such as the piano, harp, and several other instruments, do not belong to any of the established choirs. As such, the two-stave systems used for those instruments may appear with a brace line with or without a bracket. Either form of notation is acceptable, though you will likely find the brace line/bracket combination only on a formal orchestral score.

## Validation

Now that you've seen both clef systems, you may be inclined to view the contemporary system and System C as two systems fashioned along the same lines; and you may believe the contemporary method to be satisfactory. After all, the contemporary clef system does have one thing going in its favor: Almost all published music is in contemporary format. So why bother learning and using System C? Well, we'll give you *twelve* good reasons:

1) First and foremost, System C uses only *one* clef type. Even if the contemporary system shown above is embraced, it will still need to utilize *two* clef types.

2) System C clefs are all uniform in shape and size, and there are no wasted markings in the System C symbol.

3) System C clefs are much easier to notate. No fancy swirls or wiggly lines are incorporated into the symbol.

4) System C clefs are concisely informative. With a quick glance, you will determine three things: the exact octave with which you are dealing; the exact position of the tone C; and the exact pitch of that specific C tone. Regardless that the contemporary clefs are named G and F, most modern musicians don't look at either of those clefs with any great concern as to where the tones G or F are located. The once critical functions of the G clef specifically "identifying where the G is" and the F clef specifically "identifying where the F is" are, in contemporary usage, no longer critical.

5) System C clefs are easy to read. If you're concerned about having to learn to read these new clefs, don't be. The System C clef in the *high* position—with the tone C represented in the third space—is read just as the contemporary G clef is read; the System C clef in the *low* position—with the tone C represented in the second space—is read just as the contemporary F (bass) clef is read.

6) Each System C clef symbol locates *two* Cs. For example, the C5 clef symbol locates C5 by the number "5," and C4 by the lower arm of the C symbol. (Remember: The two arms of the C symbol lie precisely at the levels at which the respective ledger lines would lie.)

7) In music notated with the contemporary clefs, you may encounter G, F, and C clefs all in the same composition; when that does happen, you will likely find Cs on lines *and* spaces throughout the score. Using any System C clef symbol, the C tone always—conveniently—lies in a *space* within the stave proper.

8) The contemporary clefs respectively use one of *three* pitch indicator positions: the one suggested by the number above the clef; the one indicated by the clef itself; or the one suggested by the number below the clef. Any given System C clef uses one of only *two* pitch indicator positions.

9) Contradiction. Most of the contemporary clefs (six of them) utilize numbers above or below the clef symbol. These symbols, though easily recognizable, are technically contradictory. Why? Because in contemporary (and sensible) music notation, the use of the *8* (or *8va*) octave sign *over* a stave notated with an F clef is impermissible; and the use of the *8* (or *8va bassa*) octave sign *beneath* a stave notated with the G clef is impermissible. As such, it seems contradictory that this contemporary numbering practice is deemed acceptable for use with clef symbols yet *not* held acceptable for use with octave signs.

10) Clef change. In contemporary music, clef changes do occur. There are six movements that have come to be generally accepted: F (bass) clef to C (tenor) clef, and its reverse; F (bass) clef to G clef, and its reverse; and C (alto) clef to G clef, and its reverse. All six movements—all movements from one clef to one of an entirely different *type* and *degree*—require that the performer change his or her reading process. For example, a viola player would find the tone C on a line when employing the C (alto) clef, and find the tone C in a space when employing the G clef. The viola player, throughout a given piece of music, would have to read the staff using two different mental processes. With System C, that *doesn't* have to be the case. If the music for one performing on the viola were notated with a C4 clef, and the tones to be played went higher than the practical notational range of that clef, a change to the C5 clef would support the notational need without requiring the performer to employ a different reading process. In other words, a change from a System C *low* clef to another *low*, or a *high* to another *high*, would not only be practical but provide for easy part reading.

11) When using System C clef symbols, the tones to be played can be notated exactly at their sounded pitches. This will greatly reduce the number of octave signs and ledger lines that ordinarily would be used. Additionally, if the parts are written precisely at their sounded pitches, then certain instruments will no longer need to be classified as "transposing" instruments. Glockenspiel parts can be written using the C7 clef; piccolo and xylophone parts can be written using the C6 clef; contrabassoon and bass parts can be written using the C2 (low) clef; guitar parts can be written using the C4 (high) clef; and so forth. Yes, music for these instruments that are presently labeled "transposing" could be notated in a similar manner using the contemporary system, but the finished notated product would be less speedily and less efficiently read than the System C version would, owing to System C's neatness.

12) The contemporary system is a many-time modified system—a hand-me-down. System C, on the other hand, is brand new. Yes, it *is* a C clef, but it is much different than its precursors, and much more practical and user friendly.

## Orchestration Applications

For those of you already engrossed in music, especially those who write for one or more instruments, we offer some suggestions for and commentary on the use of the System C clefs. We list various System C clefs and the instruments' parts that might be best served by the use of those particular clefs. The list is not all inclusive or etched in stone, but it is one that may prove quite useful. Study it carefully and decide for yourself.

*Single Stave*

C2 (low): low bassoon, contrabassoon, low horn, low tuba, low cello, bass.

C3 (low): low bass clarinet, bassoon, high contrabassoon, horn, trombone, tuba, timpani, low baritone voice, bass voice, cello, high bass.

C4 (low): bass clarinet, high bassoon, high trombone, high tuba, horn, baritone voice, cello.

C5 (low): high bass clarinet, high horn, high cello.

C3: low saxophone, low guitar.

C4: low alto flute, low English horn, low clarinet, saxophone, low trumpet, low vibraphone, guitar, low mezzo-soprano voice, low alto voice, tenor voice, viola.

C5: flute, alto flute, oboe, English horn, clarinet, high saxophone, trumpet, bells, vibraphone, low xylophone, high guitar, soprano voice, mezzo-soprano voice, alto voice, high tenor voice, violin, viola.

C6: piccolo, high flute, high alto flute, high oboe, high clarinet, low glockenspiel, high vibraphone, xylophone, violin, high viola.

C7: high piccolo, glockenspiel, high xylophone, high violin.

*Staff Systems*

C7 and C5 (low): high celesta, high harp, high piano.

C6 and C4 (low): celesta, high marimba, harp, piano.

C5 and C3 (low): marimba, harp, harpsichord, piano.

C4 and C2 (low): low harp, low piano.

C5 and C3 (low) and C3 (low): organ.

Shown below are all of the sixteen System C clefs.

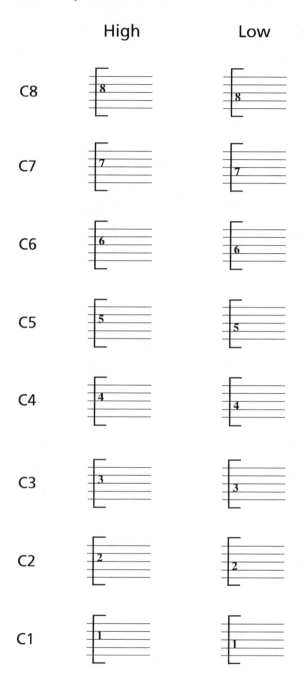

## Commentary

As mentioned earlier, certain instruments (e.g., piccolo, contrabassoon, bass) can now be written for directly at their sounded pitches. For the musician, regardless of his or her skill level, this feature takes any guesswork out of reading a line of music. Actually, parts can be written at their sounded pitches for all of the above instruments except for those that sound at a pitch *other* than that of an octave or two above or below their written parts (e.g., horn, alto flute).

With System C, one very helpful practice can easily be employed in part writing: the use of a clef of the *same* degree (*high* or *low*, that is) in more than one of the instrument's ranges. If instruments' parts were written using the System C clefs as suggested on page 24, no single instrument's part, throughout any given piece of music, would have to employ a change of clef to one of a *different* degree. For comparison, let's look at a hypothetical traditionally notated trombone part. It starts out by being written using the F (bass) clef. Later, as the line of music rises in pitch, a pitch change is necessitated. Traditionally, to accommodate the notation of those new, higher tones, the C (tenor) clef would be employed. That's fine; it will work. However, the clef change itself is radical: a change to a totally different clef—different *type* and *degree*. This can sometimes be hard to negotiate, especially for new students. With that same musical scenario, only using System C, a trombone player could start out with the C3 (low) clef and then move to the C4 (low) clef, thereby not having to use two different mental processes in reading any given line of music.

As you can see, flexibility is a key feature with System C. A trained musician performing on select instruments does not necessarily have to be subjected to radical clef changes. He or she may choose from the many System C clefs to establish the easiest process for part reading. And even if the seasoned performer does prefer clef changes that are those of changes to clefs of different degrees, he or she will still be dealing with only one clef type, one that is still easily recognizable and negotiable. For the new student, System C brings nothing but good news. In fact, in most cases, learning to read clefs of just *one* type and *one* degree may be all that the new student will ever need for clef negotiation. Additionally, for those musicians who use professional music notation software or page-layout software, System C fonts will conveniently provide for simple and concise notation of clefs.

As we've said before, it seems like it takes forever for meaninful change to take place in music theory and practice, but it doesn't have to be that way. The always-evolving musical process tells us that there *is* a consensus for simplification and facility. System C is the inevitable manifestation of a method whose time has come. Eventually realizing that System C is the superior system, musicians will embrace it and assimilate it into their everyday notational practices.

# Chapter 4

# INTERVALS

For the purpose of this book, the discussion of *intervals* is paramount. In the SPS, intervals determine the scale phrase. In *System 2000 Chord Notation*, presented later in this book, intervals and the modifications of those intervals determine the chord itself and how the chord is notated. Though this may be a subject already familiar to many musicians, this chapter is crucial for new students and helpful to those needing a quick refresher.

Before we continue, we must mention that we can not overemphasize the importance of the interval. Without the interval, we would not have *any* scales or chords. Without the interval, that invisible silence between tones, our music would not be linear; we would have only one potentially cacophonous sound. So let's take a look at the all-important interval.

## Interval

The interval, however simple and elementary, is the structure in music that harmonically provides for so many beautiful sounds. Figure 4.1 shows an example interval, the formation of which is very simple. We place one note symbol on the first (bottom) line, or staff degree. That note symbol represents the tone E. We then place another note symbol on the third line (from the bottom), directly above the first note symbol. That second note symbol represents the tone B. The difference in pitch between the two tones represented by those symbols is referred to as an *interval*. The *general* name for any interval is determined by the placement of the note symbols on the stave. The general name for the interval in figure 4.1 is a *5th* because *five* staff degrees are utilized in the formation of this interval:

line one (symbol)—space—line two—space—line three (symbol)

figure 4.1

Remember: The new C5 clef shown above is read just as the contemporary G (treble) clef is read.

The interval in figure 4.1 also has a *specific* name—a general name preceded by an adjective. The above interval's specific name is "*perfect 5th.*" The specific name is determined by how many half steps are involved in the relationship between the two tones. Though the quality of that *5th* can be changed by adding an accidental to one of the note symbols, the above interval, E-B, will always be a *5th*.

For clarity, we need to mention that in figure 4.1, the tone B itself may be referred to as a *5th*. In addition to having a letter name, a tone may have a *numerical* name. If a tone's role in an interval, chord, or scale is one of anything *other* than a *root tone* (discussed later) or tonic, the tone itself will have a numerical name (e.g., *2nd, 3rd, 4th*).

Note: To prevent any confusion in this text, we use *italics* to indicate *specific intervals* or *tones at specific intervals* (e.g., *5th, fifth*), and normal type to indicate *chords* (e.g., 5th, fifth).

Before we demonstrate how the quality of intervals can easily be changed, we must stress that just as we observe established rules in speaking and writing language, we must likewise learn to observe established rules in music notation. The set of rules regarding interval changes is *critical*. That set of rules is as follows:

1) An *augmented* interval when *raised* one half step becomes a *doubly augmented* interval.
2) A *major* or *perfect* interval when *raised* one half step becomes an *augmented* interval.
3) A *major* interval when *lowered* one half step becomes a *minor* interval.
4) A *minor* or *perfect* interval when *lowered* one half step becomes a *diminished* interval.
5) A *diminished* interval when *lowered* one half step becomes a *doubly diminished* interval.

## Simple Intervals

Next, we will take a look at the intervals used in an eight-tone scale. These are called *simple intervals* because the intervals are *within* an octave. When we work with intervals or chords, we refer to the tone that the interval or chord is "based on" (or "built on") as the *root tone*.

Figure 4.2 shows the *major* and *perfect* intervals, using the tone C as the root tone.

figure 4.2

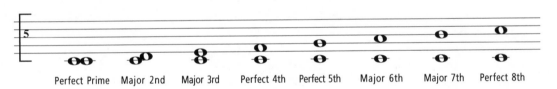

Perfect Prime    Major 2nd    Major 3rd    Perfect 4th    Perfect 5th    Major 6th    Major 7th    Perfect 8th

You can see in figure 4.2 that each interval has a specific designation. The first interval shown is referred to as a *perfect prime*, the second is referred to as a *major 2nd*, and so forth. For the sake of completeness, in figure 4.2 we have included the intervals called the *perfect prime* (which, strictly speaking, is not actually an interval) and the *perfect 8th*. However, for the balance of this book, we will exclude discussion of the *perfect prime* and *perfect 8th* intervals as they play no active role in the text of either sections of this book.

As we said earlier, we can change the quality of the interval. Let's see what happens when we take the intervals of figure 4.2 and raise the higher of the two tones of each interval one half step, according to the aforementioned rules. Figure 4.3 shows the results.

figure 4.3

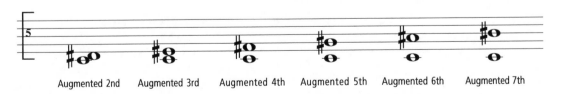

Augmented 2nd    Augmented 3rd    Augmented 4th    Augmented 5th    Augmented 6th    Augmented 7th

We see from figure 4.3 that the intervals now have their appropriately new names. We must also note here that the intervals of the *perfect 4th* and *perfect 5th* are the simple intervals that are most commonly *augmented*.

Now, let's see what happens when we take the intervals of figure 4.2 and lower the higher of the two tones of each interval one half step. Figure 4.4 shows the results.

figure 4.4

| Minor 2nd | Minor 3rd | Diminished 4th | Diminished 5th | Minor 6th | Minor 7th |

The modified intervals now have their appropriately new names.

And what would we get if we took the intervals of figure 4.4 and lowered the higher of the two tones of each interval yet another half step? Figure 4.5 shows the resulting intervals and their appropriately new names.

figure 4.5

| Diminished 2nd | Diminished 3rd | Doubly Diminished 4th | Doubly Diminished 5th | Diminished 6th | Diminished 7th |

In Chapter 6, you will see that our SPS eight-tone scale is a succession of eight different tones, with the interval between each of those tones being that of a *2nd*—either a *minor 2nd*, a *major 2nd*, or an *augmented 2nd*.

## Compound Intervals

There are large intervals that are *not* used in the eight-tone scale. These intervals—*greater* than an *octave (8th)*—are called *compound intervals*. Figure 4.6 shows three compound intervals that directly relate to the *System 2000 Chord Notation* section of this book—the *major 9th*, the *major 11th*, and the *major 13th*.

figure 4.6

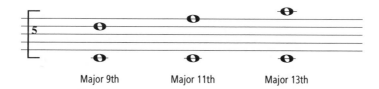

| Major 9th | Major 11th | Major 13th |

If we took the intervals of figure 4.6 and raised the higher of the two tones of each of those intervals one half step, we would have those of figure 4.7.

figure 4.7

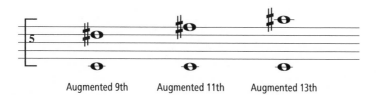

| Augmented 9th | Augmented 11th | Augmented 13th |

And, if we took the intervals of figure 4.6 and lowered the higher of the two tones of each of those intervals one half step, we would have those of figure 4.8.

figure 4.8

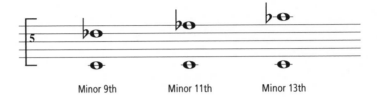

Minor 9th          Minor 11th          Minor 13th

## Relative Position

Figure 4.9 demonstrates two like intervals: two *major 3rds*, E-G♯ and F-A. As the respective root tones, E and F, are one half step apart, these intervals may be referred to as *adjacent* (or *successive*) intervals.

figure 4.9

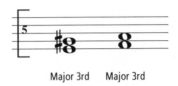

Major 3rd     Major 3rd

Figure 4.10 demonstrates two like intervals: two *major 3rds*, C-E and E-G♯. As the top note, E, of the first interval is the same as the bottom note of the second interval, these intervals may be referred to as *contiguous* intervals.

figure 4.10

Major 3rd     Major 3rd

## Half Steps

The following list features twenty simple intervals and the number of half steps constituent in those intervals.

| Interval | Half Steps | Interval | Half Steps |
|---|---|---|---|
| *minor 2nd* | 1 | *diminished 5th* | 6 |
| *major 2nd* | 2 | *perfect 5th* | 7 |
| *diminished 3rd* | 2 | *diminished 6th* | 7 |
| *augmented 2nd* | 3 | *augmented 5th* | 8 |
| *minor 3rd* | 3 | *minor 6th* | 8 |
| *major 3rd* | 4 | *major 6th* | 9 |
| *diminished 4th* | 4 | *diminished 7th* | 9 |
| *augmented 3rd* | 5 | *augmented 6th* | 10 |
| *perfect 4th* | 5 | *minor 7th* | 10 |
| *augmented 4th* | 6 | *major 7th* | 11 |

# The Scale Phrase System

## Chapter 5

## THE SCALE PHRASE

The Scale Phrase System (SPS), to a degree, resembles the old, traditional tetrachord system. A tetrachord, by strict definition, is a group of four successive tones that have an interval of a *perfect 4th* from the first tone to the fourth tone. You will recall from Chapter 4 that the interval of a *perfect 4th* is one of *five* half steps. To form a scale with the tetrachord system, two tetrachords are conjoined. Likewise, to form a scale, the SPS conjoins two four-tone groups, each of those groups being a *scale phrase*. With the scale phrase, however, the intervallic criterion of the *perfect 4th* does *not* apply. The scale phrase, from the first tone to the fourth tone, can have *four* to *six* half steps and still maintain its integrity as a scale phrase. This flexibility allows for precise and orderly construction of eight-tone scales. Let's take a look at how it works.

A *scale phrase* is a group of four successive tones used in ascending or descending order. Between each of those tones is a distance known as an interval. In the examples in this text, "H" indicates one half step, "W" (whole step) indicates two half steps, and "3H" indicates three half steps. The order of the intervals between the four *ascending* successive tones is that which determines the *type* of scale phrase. Figure 5.1 shows an example: the **major** scale phrase, the first of the eight basic scale phrases.

figure 5.1

| tones: | C | | D | | E | | F |
|--------|---|---|---|---|---|---|---|
| intervals: | | W | | W | | H | |

Note here the intervals: The interval between C and D is one whole step; the interval between D and E is one whole step; and the interval between E and F is one half step. In this example, it is clearly shown that the intervals occurring in the ascending order of "W  W  H" determine the **major** scale phrase. The **major** scale phrase may be referred to as a *five*-half-step scale phrase.

Figure 5.2 shows the **major** scale phrase in descending order. Though the order of the intervals is the reverse of that shown in figure 5.1, the four successive tones still constitute a **major** scale phrase. Remember: The order of the intervals between the four *ascending* successive tones is that which determines the type of scale phrase.

figure 5.2

| tones: | F | | E | | D | | C |
|--------|---|---|---|---|---|---|---|
| intervals: | | H | | W | | W | |

The **major** scale phrase, our first scale phrase, is a *five*-half-step scale phrase. This scale phrase is identical to the ascending "W-W-H" tetrachord of the Middle Ages. Two **major** scale phrases can be conjoined to form a popular and highly serviceable scale.

## Major

```
C       D       E       F
    W       W       H
```

The **minor** scale phrase is a *five*-half-step scale phrase.

## Minor

```
D       E       F       G
    W       H       W
```

The **minor 2** scale phrase is a *five*-half-step scale phrase.

## Minor 2

```
E       F       G       A
    H       W       W
```

The **augmented** scale phrase is a *six*-half-step scale phrase. The third whole step in this phrase gives it a sort of "uplifting" feel (in the example below, the rise from the tones A to B). This **augmented** scale phrase, however, with its *three* whole step intervals, is in fact too "strong," so to speak, to be combined with another **augmented**. Such a combination (including the bridge step) would create a scale with *thirteen* half steps, which would disqualify it from being an eight-tone scale, or any ordinary scale for that matter. We also need to validate one important characteristic of this scale phrase—its name. We could conveniently call this the "whole step" scale phrase. However, we have not done so for three reasons: (1) Regarding the terminology used in the SPS (mostly traditional or contemporary terminology used a bit differently), the term **augmented** fits in quite neatly: It works well logically and mechanically with the other scale phrase names; (2) To keep the introduction of new terms to an absolute minimum, we use the term **augmented**, a term which has been used in music for centuries; and (3) Though admittedly this scale phrase does indeed have three "whole step" intervals, we use the term **augmented** to prevent confusion later on when we discuss the Whole Step Scale, a scale which is *not* an eight-tone scale.

## Augmented

```
F       G       A       B
    W       W       W
```

The **diminished** scale phrase is a *four*-half-step scale phrase. The **diminished** scale phrase, by virtue of its two half steps, is a "weak" scale phrase, so to speak. It is not used often, and when it is used, it is usually combined with the **augmented**, the strongest scale phrase. This combination seemingly provides balance.

The **harmonic** scale phrase is a *five*-half-step scale phrase. Traditionally, the interval of three half steps (the *augmented 2nd*) had sometimes been viewed as being melodically awkward; however, in actuality, it is very interesting, and, if not used excessively, can be pleasing to the ear.

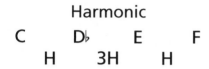

The **altered** scale phrase is a *six*-half-step scale phrase. This scale phrase features all of the permissible scale phrase intervals—H, W, and 3H. To adhere to our policy of avoiding the use of new terms, if possible, we refer to this peculiar scale phrase by the term **altered**. We think of this scale phrase as an altered **minor** scale phrase; that is, the fourth tone of the scale phrase is chromatically altered (the tone F in the example below). In Chapter Seven, we demonstrate four scales that use this scale phrase. As those scales have been around for a very long time, we feel that we would be remiss in excluding them from demonstration.

### Altered

C       D       E♭       F♯
  W     H     3H

The **blues** scale phrase is a *six*-half-step scale phrase. This intriguing scale phrase is the second basic scale phrase that features all of the permissible scale phrase intervals. Ordinarily, we *don't* use this scale phrase to form discrete scales, the notable exception being that of combining the **blues** scale phrase with the **unusual 7** scale phrase (shown on page 36); this combination (in the key of C, for example) will form a peculiar but workable scale: C, D♯, E♯, F♯, G, A♯, B, C

This scale phrase is noteworthy because the **blues** scale phrase has an *enharmonic* form: C, E♭, F, F♯ (the notation is different but the sound is ultimately the same). This enharmonic form plays a prominent role in the seven-tone version of the Blues Scale (a non-eight-tone scale discussed in Chapter 9); and it also plays a prominent role in melodies employed in the Blues style of music.

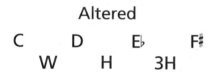

Now that we are familiar with the eight basic scale phrases, let's arrange them to be viewed for comparison.

## Major

| C | | D | | E | | F |
|---|---|---|---|---|---|---|
| | W | | W | | H | |

## Minor

| C | | D | | E♭ | | F |
|---|---|---|---|---|---|---|
| | W | | H | | W | |

## Minor 2

| C | | D♭ | | E♭ | | F |
|---|---|---|---|---|---|---|
| | H | | W | | W | |

## Augmented

| C | | D | | E | | F♯ |
|---|---|---|---|---|---|---|
| | W | | W | | W | |

## Diminished

| C | | D♭ | | E♭ | | F♭ |
|---|---|---|---|---|---|---|
| | H | | W | | H | |

## Harmonic

| C | | D♭ | | E | | F |
|---|---|---|---|---|---|---|
| | H | | 3H | | H | |

## Altered

| C | | D | | E♭ | | F♯ |
|---|---|---|---|---|---|---|
| | W | | H | | 3H | |

## Blues

| C | | D♯ | | E♯ | | F♯ |
|---|---|---|---|---|---|---|
| | 3H | | W | | H | |

Also, you should repeatedly play these scale phrases on your instrument in order to get a feel for each of these. You will find that they are quickly and easily memorized. Even if you already know scales and some theory, repeated playing of these scale phrases will help you develop the ability to mentally identify the scale phrases within the scales that you use. Shown below are the eight basic scale phrases as played in the key of C.

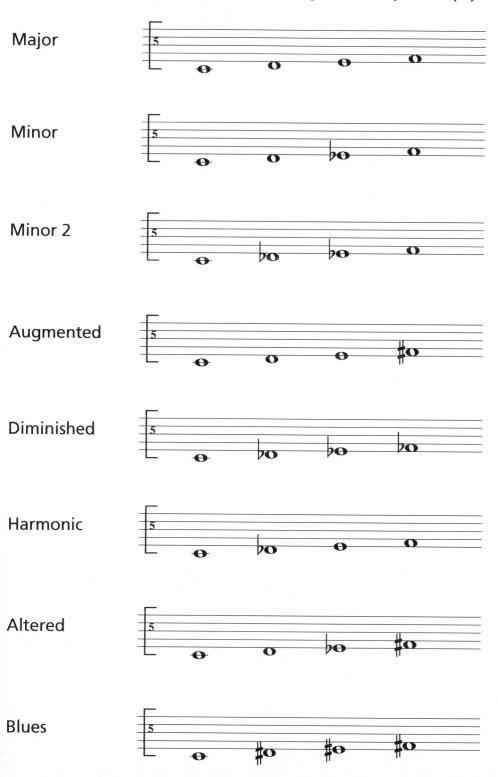

For the sake of completeness, we show the other eight tone combinations that qualify as scale phrases. These scale phrases, however, are most unusual; accordingly, we label them with the term *Unusual*.

### Unusual 1

C      Db      Ebb      Fb
   H     H     W

### Unusual 2

C      Db      Ebb      F
   H     H    3H

### Unusual 3

C      Db      Eb      F#
   H     W    3H

### Unusual 4

C      Db      E      F#
   H    3H     W

### Unusual 5

C      D      Eb      Fb
   W     H     H

### Unusual 6

C      D      E#      F#
   W    3H     H

### Unusual 7

C      D#      E      F
 3H     H     H

### Unusual 8

C      D#      E      F#
 3H     H     W

# Chapter 6

# SCALE CONSTRUCTION

Now that you are familiar with the eight basic scale phrases, you can use them to construct scales, to analyze existing scales that you commonly use, or to enhance your compositions.

The process of building an eight-tone scale using scale phrases is very simple. All you need are two suitable scale phrases and a *bridge step*. A bridge step is nothing more than the interval that exists between the two scale phrases. The bridge step can be one half step, one whole step (two half steps), or three half steps. It may *not* be more than three half steps.

As an example, let's build an eight-tone scale using two **major** scale phrases. Figure 6.1 shows the combination.

figure 6.1

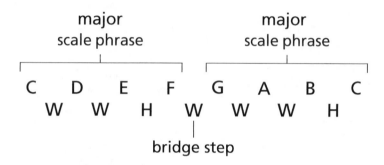

You can see that the total number of half steps in this scale is *twelve*. This scale, which satisfies the definition given in Chapter 2, is an eight-tone scale. As you will discover later, the scale formed in figure 6.1 is the C Major Scale.

Let's look at another example combination. Figure 6.2 shows the scale formed by combining one **augmented** scale phrase and one **major** scale phrase.

figure 6.2

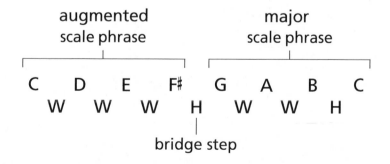

As you can see, we have built an eight-tone scale. The bridge step in this scale is that of *one half step*, not one whole step. If the bridge step were one whole step (or even three half steps), the total number of half steps in the scale would exceed twelve, which is not permissible. As you will discover in the next chapter, the scale that we have just formed is the C Augmented Major Scale, though in the SPS, we may simply refer to this scale as the C Augmented Scale.

Now we must demonstrate one of the few exceptions in the SPS, an exception that applies specifically to the *combination* of scale phrases. There are a few scale phrase combinations that are *not* acceptable as eight-tone scales. Figure 6.3 shows one of those combinations—a **diminished** with another **diminished**. Figuratively speaking, the **diminished** scale phrase is too weak to be combined with another **diminished**.

figure 6.3

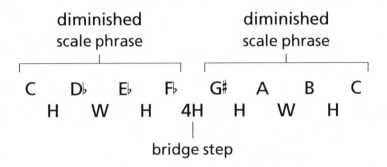

This combination of scale phrases fails because it effects the impractical four-half-step bridge step, a bridge step which spans a distance equivalent to an entire scale phrase.

Figure 6.4 shows that if we changed the unacceptable bridge step in figure 6.3 to one that is *three* half steps, we would have created another unacceptable condition: a scale that does not extend from the tonic to the octave.

figure 6.4

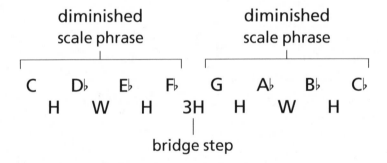

The other unacceptable scale phrase combinations are those of any combination of **augmenteds**, **altereds**, or **blues**. Again, figuratively speaking, each of those three types of scale phrases is too strong to be combined with another of the same kind or with any of the other two kinds.

Regarding the method used in naming SPS scales, we'd like to emphasize our particular use of terms. In Chapter 7, you will be introduced to many SPS scale names that use *two* terms rather than one. In the scale name Augmented Minor, for example, the name denotes a structure made of two distinct scale phrases, ordered **augmented** first and **minor** second. In this scale name, the term Augmented is used to clearly denote that the first scale phrase is an **augmented** scale phrase. Here, the term Augmented is *not* used in the grammatically conventional sense; that is, the term Augmented is *not* used as an adjective modifying the term Minor.

# Chapter 7

# SCALE DESCRIPTIONS

With the SPS, scale construction and order are surprisingly clear. This chapter describes which scales are formed when two specific scale phrases are conjoined, and it explains why most of these existing scales have been assigned new SPS names.

Demonstrated below are select SPS eight-tone scales. Each of the scales listed below is in the key of C, meaning that the tonic (or key tone) of that scale is C; or in the case of the corresponding mode, the final is C. Additionally, if a scale has a directly corresponding mode name, that name is also listed (scale name/mode name).

## Major / Ionian

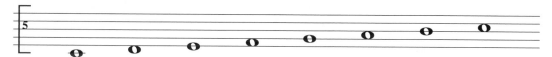

The Major Scale is constructed with two **major** scale phrases. This scale is the same as the Ionian mode, the mode built on the first scale degree of the Major Scale.

Recalling the procedure from Chapter 2, you will see that this Ionian mode is created by using *only* the tones of the C Major Scale (*this* scale, in fact), and building a mode on the first tone of that scale—the tone C. Obviously then, the C Major Scale and the Ionian in this case—the Ionian of C—are technically the same.

## Minor / Dorian

The Minor Scale is constructed with two **minor** scale phrases. This scale is the same as the Dorian mode, the mode built on the second scale degree of the Major Scale.

This mode *is* the Dorian mode; however, we must stress here that it is specifically the Dorian of B♭. The example scale shown above is in the key of C, but functioning as a mode, it is *not* the Dorian of C. To create the above mode, you would take the B♭ Major Scale (*only* those scale tones) and start a mode on the *second* tone of that scale. The resulting mode would be the Dorian mode—the Dorian of B♭.

## Minor 2 / Phrygian

The Minor 2 Scale is constructed with two **minor 2** scale phrases. This scale is the same as the Phrygian mode, the mode built on the third scale degree of the Major Scale.

## Augmented / Lydian

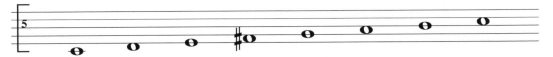

The Augmented Scale is constructed with one **augmented** scale phrase and one **major** scale phrase. This scale is the same as the Lydian mode, the mode built on the fourth scale degree of the Major Scale.

As constructed with scale phrases, this is the Augmented Major Scale; however, in the SPS, it is acceptable to refer to this scale by its nickname—the Augmented Scale. Though the single term Augmented implies the use of two **augmented** scale phrases, we know from Chapters 5 and 6 that the combination of two **augmented** scale phrases does not qualify as an SPS eight-tone scale; in this case, the second scale phrase, the **major** scale phrase, is the default scale phrase, so to speak. There are only a few nicknames and shortcuts promoted in the SPS, and those that are promoted should prove to be helpful.

Contemporary names for this scale are Lydian, Lydian Major, and Major #4. The name Major #4 is an especially poor name. This contemporary name suggests that the fourth tone of the scale has the sharp accidental (♯) applied to it. If one were referring to the C Major Scale with the fourth tone "sharped," the #4 designation (C, D, E, F♯, G, A, B, C) would be appropriate; that could correctly be called the C Major #4 Scale. However, using the #4 designation for the Major #4 Scale works *only* on scales that start on the tones C, D, E, F♯, G, A, and B. To construct a Major #4 Scale starting on C♭, C♯, D♭, E♭, F, G♭, A♭, or B♭, the #4 method would be improper. For example, if you took the D♭ Major Scale and sharped the fourth tone, that tone would be G♯; consequently, you would *not* have formed the intended D♭ Major #4 Scale, for the correct fourth tone of the so-called D♭ Major #4 Scale is G (natural), *not* G♯.

## Major Minor / Mixolydian

The Major Minor Scale is constructed with one **major** scale phrase and one **minor** scale phrase. This scale is the same as the Mixolydian mode, the mode built on the fifth scale degree of the Major Scale.

Contemporary names for this scale are Mixolydian and Dominant, the name Dominant being chosen because the scale steps of that scale are the same as those of a mode started on the *dominant* (5th scale degree) of a Major scale. The name Dominant Scale, however, suggests the mix of two schools of thought, because the word "dominant" is relative to *scales* while the tones employed in the Dominant Scale are *modal*. So, until the student becomes more deeply immersed in theory and fully grasps the tonic-dominant relationship, his or her use of the classification Major Minor Scale will prove to be simpler and more direct (and, perhaps, permanent).

## Minor 3 / Aeolian

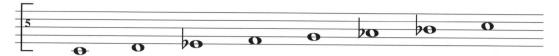

The Minor 3 Scale is constructed with one **minor** scale phrase and one **minor 2** scale phrase. This scale is the same as the Aeolian mode, the mode built on the sixth scale degree of the Major Scale.

As constructed with scale phrases, this is the Minor Minor 2 Scale; however, we simply refer to this scale as the Minor 3 Scale, for this scale is a combination of the **minor** and **minor 2** scale phrases, and it is the *third* of the basic *minor* scales (i.e., the modes built on the Major Scale using *only* **minor** and/or **minor 2** scale phrases).

One contemporary name for this scale is Aeolian. The traditional name for this scale is Natural (or Pure) Minor. If, for example, you were to take the tones of the C Major Scale (all white keys on the piano) and build a mode starting on the tone A, you would have built the Aeolian mode—specifically, the Aeolian of C. This mode is the mode that eventually went on to be called the Natural Minor Scale. The tones of our example, the A Natural Minor Scale, are A, B, C, D, E, F, G, and A. Even without a knowledge of harmonics (fundamentals, partials, etc.), you would likely intuitively perceive that sequence of tones as a "minor" one; and by virtue of how those tones and intervals can be conveniently drawn from the C Major Scale, you might be inclined to call that scale a sort of "natural" one. However, as a scale, it is not structurally natural. The SPS Minor and Minor 2 Scales are certainly more natural (and uniform): The Minor Scale is constructed with *only* **minor** scale phrases, and the Minor 2 Scale is constructed with *only* **minor 2** scale phrases. Even if you were to use the old tetrachord system, the case would be the same. Additionally, as a mode or even a variation of one of the four original modes, the Aeolian is neither totally natural nor original: It was not formally introduced and accepted until sometime in the 1500s, no less than 900 years after the original four modes surfaced.

When analyzing the Minor 3 Scale (the traditional Natural Minor Scale, or Aeolian mode) and the Major Scale (Ionian mode), some modern music theorists might classify these two scales as the *diatonic scales*, a subset of what might be referred to as the *prime scales* (see page 64).

## Minor 2 Augmented / Locrian

The Minor 2 Augmented Scale is constructed with one **minor 2** scale phrase and one **augmented** scale phrase. This scale is the same as the Locrian mode, the mode built on the seventh scale degree of the Major Scale. For this scale, we allow the use of its mode-derived nickname—Locrian Scale.

Contemporary names for this scale are Locrian and Half-diminished. The name Half-diminished resulted from the mixing of two schools of thought. For the beginner in music theory, that contemporary name may cause confusion, especially if the beginner does not have an understanding of chord construction and chord notation.

## Minor Major / Mysian

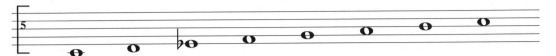

The Minor Major Scale is constructed with one **minor** scale phrase and one **major** scale phrase. This scale is the same as the Mysian mode, the mode built on the first scale degree of the Minor Major Scale (this scale, of course).

Contemporary names for this scale are Melodic Minor, Jazz Minor, and Dorian ♮7. The Melodic Minor Scale has an *ascending* and a *descending* version. Classical musicians have employed one or both of the versions; Jazz musicians have ordinarily employed only the ascending version. Our SPS Minor Major Scale discussed here is actually the same as the *ascending* version of the traditional Melodic Minor Scale.

It is interesting to note that the traditional "minor" scales have a seemingly long, drawn-out history. At some point in the 1500s, the **Aeolian mode** was formally acknowledged, and it quickly became recognized as the **Natural Minor Scale**, the first minor scale (historically, that is). In this discussion, we'll use the tones and inherent intervals of the A Natural Minor Scale as our example.

At some point after the establishment of the Natural Minor Scale, someone determined that the interval of the leading tone (G) to the octave of the tonic (A) should be one *half step*, not one whole step, so that the leading tone would more smoothly lead to the octave of the tonic. So, to smooth out that scale, the *seventh* scale degree was raised one half step. This altered Natural Minor Scale (A, B, C, D, E, F, G♯, and A) was then called the **Harmonic Minor Scale**. This scale was widely used for nearly two centuries until another major alteration was made.

At some point in the 1700s, composers came to general agreement that the Harmonic Minor Scale would ascend more smoothly if its *sixth* scale degree were raised one half step (A, B, C, D, E, F♯, G♯, and A). They felt, however, that the scale's descent would sound smoother if the tones were played in their "natural" position, just as in the Natural Minor Scale. This altered scale, then, was called the **Melodic Minor Scale**.

So, there you have it. The Aeolian Mode became the Natural Minor Scale, which begat the Harmonic Minor Scale, which begat the Melodic Minor Scale. Yes, this is a very rough description of what happened historically, but it should adequately help you visualize the evolution of the commonly used traditional minor scales. Though we do not consider the Natural Minor Scale "natural" in the strictest sense of the word, we do admit that the Natural Minor Scale, as the Aeolian mode, was indeed used before the 1500s. However, regardless of when the Aeolian mode made its quiet debut, we do find it incredible that it took literally *hundreds* of years for the Aeolian mode or Natural Minor Scale to be musically metamorphosed into the Melodic Minor. With the SPS, however, you won't have to wait that long. *Our* minor scales are immediately ready to be used—and easy to learn!

## Minor 2 Minor / Pamphrylian

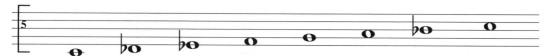

The Minor 2 Minor Scale is constructed with one **minor 2** scale phrase and one **minor** scale phrase. This scale is the same as the Pamphrylian mode, the mode built on the second scale degree of the Minor Major Scale.

Contemporary names for this scale are Dorian ♭2, Dorian ♭9, and Javanese. This scale is not commonly used.

## Augmented 2 / Galatian

The Augmented 2 Scale is constructed with one **augmented** scale phrase and one **diminished** scale phrase. This scale is the same as the Galatian mode, the mode built on the third scale degree of the Minor Major Scale.

As constructed with scale phrases (one **augmented** and one **diminished**), this is the Augmented Diminished Scale. This scale employs *both* of the two most commonly augmented simple intervals—the *4th* and the *5th*. For this scale, we allow the nickname Augmented 2 Scale. In the SPS, we view the Augmented Scale (page 40) and the Augmented 2 Scale as "sister" scales.

Contemporary names for this scale are Lydian ♯5 and Lydian Augmented.

## Augmented Minor / Lycian

The Augmented Minor Scale is constructed with one **augmented** scale phrase and one **minor** scale phrase. This scale is the same as the Lycian mode, the mode built on the fourth scale degree of the Minor Major Scale.

Contemporary names for this scale are Lydian ♭7, Lydian Dominant, Mixolydian ♯4, Mixolydian ♯11, and Overtone. As we mentioned before, for those not yet deeply immersed in traditional or contemporary theory, the contemporary names will likely prove to be confusing. The Augmented Minor Scale is the same as the Augmented Scale with one exception—the interval from the first to the seventh tone of the scale is an interval of a *minor 7th* (10 half steps). This scale has the prominent feature of the Augmented Scale (the *augmented 4th*) and the prominent feature of the Major Minor Scale (the *minor 7th*). As the frequently used contemporary name Lydian Dominant indicates the blend of two different theoretical approaches, it stands that using the name Augmented Minor (from its constituent scale phrases) is simpler and more accurate.

## Major Minor 2 / Bithynian

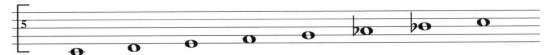

The Major Minor 2 Scale is constructed with one **major** scale phrase and one **minor 2** scale phrase. This scale is the same as the Bithynian mode, the mode built on the fifth scale degree of the Minor Major Scale.

Contemporary names for this scale are Melodic Major, Mixolydian ♭6, Mixolydian ♭13, Hindu, and Bartok.

## Minor Augmented / Carian

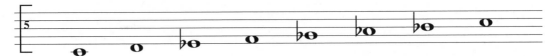

The Minor Augmented Scale is constructed with one **minor** scale phrase and one **augmented** scale phrase. This scale is the same as the Carian mode, the mode built on the sixth scale degree of the Minor Major Scale. For this scale, we allow the use of the mode-derived nickname Locrian M2 Scale. In the SPS, we view the Locrian Scale and the Locrian M2 Scale as "sister" scales.

Contemporary names for this scale are Semi-Locrian, Locrian ♮2, Locrian ♮9, and Locrian ♯2. The contemporary name Locrian ♮2 is appropriate *only* in the cases of Locrian ♮2 scales built on C, D, E♭, F, G, A, and B♭. In all of the remaining scales, the respective second tone would not be notated as a natural tone.

The contemporary name Locrian ♯2 implies that the second tone of the scale has the sharp accidental (♯) applied to it. The ♯2 designation, however, is vague and misleading, and is technically improper. In the so-called Locrian ♯2 Scale, the sharp symbol applied to the second tone would be appropriate *only* in the cases of the Locrian ♯2 Scales built on C♯, E, F♯, and B. Even so, of those four tones, E is the only commonly used scale key.

Let's look at a prime example of the inappropriate ♯2 designation for this scale: To form the C Locrian ♯2 Scale in the contemporary sense, meaning without using scale phrases, we would have to start with the C Locrian Scale. The ♯2 designation would strongly suggest that we apply the sharp accidental to the second tone of that Locrian Scale. If we did "sharp" the second tone, the resultant tones would be C, D♯, E♭, F, G♭, A♭, B♭, and C. That is *not* the intended scale, whether we call it C Locrian ♯2 or C Locrian M2. The actual intention of whoever designed the original Locrian ♯2 Scale was to have us "raise the tone at the interval of the *2nd* (of the Locrian Scale) one half step." That's all. If we did just that, the resultant tones would be C, D, E♭, F, G♭, A♭, B♭, and C. We can clearly see that in the contemporary Locrian ♯2 Scale, the interval between the first and second tone is to be that of a *major 2nd*; however, the name Locrian ♯2 is vague.

## Diminished Augmented / Cilician

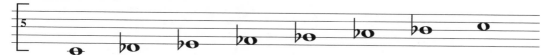

Though the very name of this scale may sound like a contradiction, this is indeed the Diminished Augmented Scale. This scale is constructed with one **diminished** scale phrase and one **augmented** scale phrase. This scale is the same as the Cilician mode, the mode built on the seventh scale degree of the Minor Major Scale.

Contemporary names for this scale are Super Locrian, Diminished Whole Tone, Locrian ♭4, and Altered. From the SPS standpoint, the name Diminished Whole Step could have merit, for the **augmented** scale phrase does indeed have *all* whole step intervals. However, in light of what we briefly touched on in Chapters 2 and 5 (specifically regarding the term "whole step"), naming this scale directly from its constituent scale phrases proves to be more accurate and concise.

## Harmonic

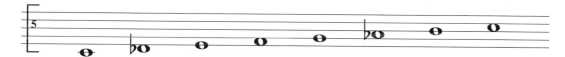

The Harmonic Scale is constructed with two **harmonic** scale phrases.

Contemporary names for this scale are Double Harmonic Major, Ionian ♭2 ♭6, Byzantine, and Gypsy. Regardless of the reasoning behind choosing the name Double Harmonic Major, naming this scale including the term *major* is both confusing and misleading. This scale does not contain any **major** scale phrases (*or* tetrachords, if viewed from the traditional standpoint), so referring to this scale as the Harmonic Scale is mechanically and logically sound.

## Major Harmonic

The Major Harmonic Scale is constructed with one **major** scale phrase and one **harmonic** scale phrase.

Contemporary names for this scale are Ionian ♭6 and Harmonic Major.

The Major Harmonic Scale is *enharmonically* the same as the contemporary Ionian ♯5 Scale (C, D, E, F, G♯, A, B, C), a scale that is the same as the mode built on the third scale degree of the traditional Harmonic Minor Scale (the SPS Minor Harmonic Scale). However, due to the intervals between their respective tones, they are actually different scales. The SPS name for the Ionian ♯5 Scale is Major Diminished.

For this scale, as the scale phrases are in the order of **major** first and **harmonic** second, the name Major Harmonic appropriately seems to be the name of choice.

### Minor Harmonic

The Minor Harmonic Scale is constructed with one **minor** scale phrase and one **harmonic** scale phrase.

Contemporary names for this scale are Harmonic Minor, Aeolian ♮7, and Mohammedan. The name Harmonic Minor is similar to our SPS name; however, as the scale phrases are in the order of **minor** first and **harmonic** second, the name Minor Harmonic appropriately seems to be the name of choice.

### Harmonic Minor 2

The Harmonic Minor 2 Scale is constructed with one **harmonic** scale phrase and one **minor 2** scale phrase. This scale is the same as the mode built on the fifth scale degree of the Minor Harmonic Scale.

Contemporary names for this scale are Mixolydian ♭2 ♭6, Mixolydian ♭9 ♭13, Phrygian Dominant, Spanish Phrygian, and Spanish Gypsy. This is a mode used in Arabic or Turkish music, sometimes referred to as the Hijaz-Nahawand Scale (Hijaz: first four tones; Nahawand: second four tones); it's also a mode used in Jewish music, sometimes referred to as the Ahavoh Rabboh Scale.

### Altered Harmonic

The Altered Harmonic Scale is constructed with one **altered** scale phrase and one **harmonic** scale phrase. This scale is the same as the mode built on the fourth scale degree of the Harmonic Scale.

Contemporary names for this scale are Hungarian Minor, Harmonic Minor ♯4, Double Harmonic Minor, Lydian ♭3 ♭6, and Algerian. Despite the fact that the term *minor* is used in three of those names, this scale contains no **minor** scale phrases.

### Altered Major

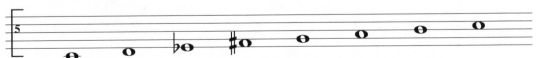

The Altered Major Scale is constructed with one **altered** scale phrase and one **major** scale phrase. This scale is the same as the mode built on the fourth scale degree of the Major Harmonic Scale.

Contemporary names for this scale are Lydian ♭3, Jazz Minor ♯4, and Jazz Minor ♯11.

## Altered Minor

The Altered Minor Scale is constructed with one **altered** scale phrase and one **minor** scale phrase. This scale is the same as the mode built on the fourth scale degree of the Minor Harmonic Scale.

Contemporary names for this scale are Romanian Minor, Dorian ♯4, and Dorian ♯11.

## Altered Minor 2

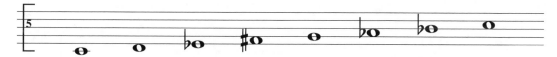

The Altered Minor 2 Scale is constructed with one **altered** scale phrase and one **minor 2** scale phrase. This scale is the same as the mode built on the fourth scale degree of the Minor 2 Harmonic Scale (shown below).

Contemporary names for this scale are Hungarian Gypsy and Aeolian ♯4.

## Minor 2 Major

The Minor 2 Major Scale is constructed with one **minor 2** scale phrase and one **major** scale phrase.

Contemporary names for this scale are Neapolitan Major and Jazz Minor ♭2.

## Minor 2 Harmonic

The Minor 2 Harmonic Scale is constructed with one **minor 2** scale phrase and one **harmonic** scale phrase.

Contemporary names for this scale are Neapolitan Minor and Harmonic Minor ♭2.

## Augmented Minor 2

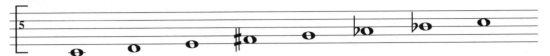

The Augmented Minor 2 Scale is constructed with one **augmented** scale phrase and one **minor 2** scale phrase. This scale is the same as the mode built on the fourth scale degree of the Minor 2 Major Scale.

Contemporary names for this scale are Lydian ♭6 ♭7, Lydian Dominant ♭6, and Lydian Minor.

## Major Augmented

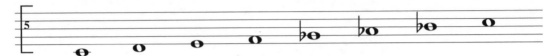

The Major Augmented Scale is constructed with one **major** scale phrase and one **augmented** scale phrase. This scale is the same as the mode built on the fifth scale degree of the Minor 2 Major Scale.

Contemporary names for this scale are Major Locrian, Mixolydian ♭5 ♭6, and Arabian.

## Scale Names

Over the past several decades, the names of some of the contemporary scales have been changed, and those names were changed even though the scales' respective structures had not changed. We believe that they were changed because musicians evolve and are always looking for something better, something more precise. However, the problem that we mentioned at the outset of this book still remains. Renaming or reclassifying while conceptually remaining within the context of the existing method will often involve the blending of different schools of thought. That blending may prove useful at first, but as the blending is allowed to continue, and as new features or ideas are assimilated into the mix, confusion will likely result.

For example, take the SPS Augmented Minor Scale. This scale has several contemporary names, each of which has, in turn, been the favored contemporary name for that particular scale. As of this writing, the name Lydian ♭7 seems to be the favored name. If the SPS scale names are not ultimately embraced and inculcated, that name could conceivably hold for a very long time; or, it may, after a surprisingly short amount of time, drop by the wayside. We don't know. But we do know that simply changing scales' respective names every so often does not create a genuine "system." On the contrary, random revision ordinarily hinders the establishment of a sound and lasting method.

To further demonstrate our point, take the contemporary Melodic Major Scale. As of this writing, favored names are Mixolydian ♭6 and Mixolydian ♭13. With the "♭6" designation, the novice might assume that this is the Mixolydian Scale with its sixth scale degree lowered one half step; as the complete Mixolydian Scale (or mode) is comprised of eight tones, this assumption is reasonable. But how would the novice negotiate the "♭13" designation? He or she would not know that the theorist was referring to either (a) the tone at the interval of a *13th* above the tonic, thereby suggesting the scale's relation to "chord structure," or (b) the 13th partial of the harmonic series, thereby suggesting the physics-determined "natural" inclusion of that tone in the scale.

With the SPS eight-tone scales presented here, no one will need to change the names every so often. With the SPS—an actual system—the scales are simply and concisely named using only one or two applicable terms. When you choose an SPS scale, you know exactly what you are getting.

# Chapter 8

# EIGHT-TONE SCALES

For comparison and scrutiny, we will now display twenty-two of the eight-tone scales demonstrated in the last chapter. This way you will be better able to visualize the similarities of and differences between the scales. All of the examples below are in the key of C. The first seven scales shown are the modes of the Major Scale.

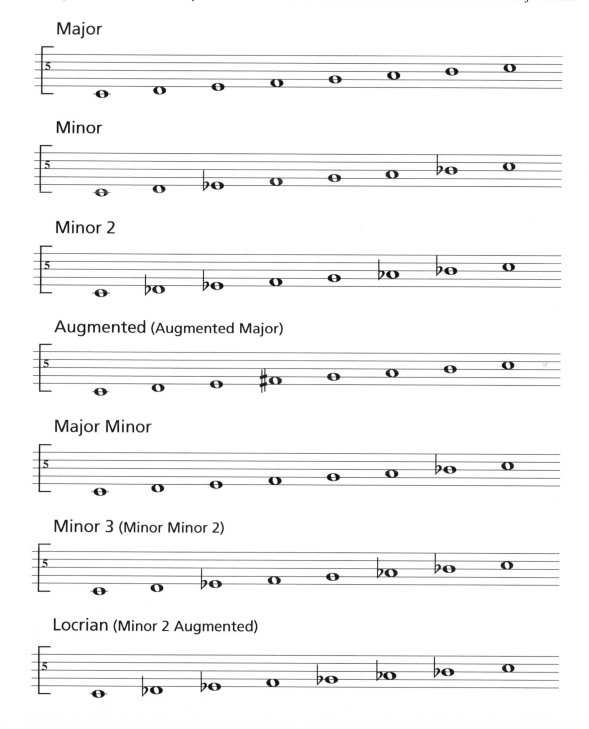

The next seven scales shown are the modes of the Minor Major Scale.

## Minor Major

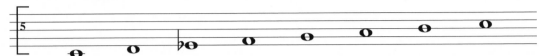

## Minor 2 Minor

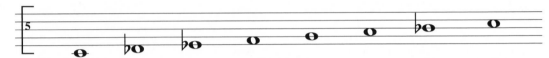

## Augmented 2 (Augmented Diminished)

## Augmented Minor

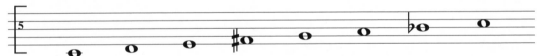

## Major Minor 2

## Locrian M2 (Minor Augmented)

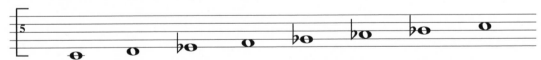

## Diminished Augmented

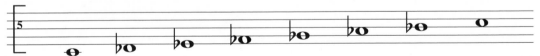

## Harmonic

## Minor Harmonic

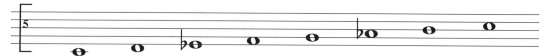

## Major Harmonic

## Harmonic Minor 2

## Altered Harmonic

## Altered Major

## Altered Minor

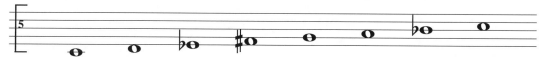

## Altered Minor 2

## Possibilities

Shown below are the fifty-four permissible basic scale phrase combinations. In this text, twenty-six of those combinations are demonstrated. The combinations not shown in this text will rarely be seen in modern music, but they are available if needed.

Major Major
Major Minor
Major Minor 2
Major Augmented
Major Diminished
Major Harmonic
Major Altered
Major Blues

Minor Major
Minor Minor
Minor Minor 2
Minor Augmented
Minor Diminished
Minor Harmonic
Minor Altered
Minor Blues

Minor 2 Major
Minor 2 Minor
Minor 2 Minor 2
Minor 2 Augmented
Minor 2 Diminished
MInor 2 Harmonic
Minor 2 Altered
Minor 2 Blues

Augmented Major
Augmented Minor
Augmented Minor 2
Augmented Diminished
Augmented Harmonic

Diminished Major
Diminished Minor
Diminished Minor 2
Diminished Augmented
Diminished Harmonic
Diminished Altered
Diminished Blues

Harmonic Major
Harmonic Minor
Harmonic Minor 2
Harmonic Augmented
Harmonic Diminished
Hamonic Harmonic
Harmonic Altered
Harmonic Blues

Altered Major
Altered Minor
Altered Minor 2
Altered Diminished
Altered Harmonic

Blues Major
Blues Minor
Blues Minor 2
Blues Diminished
Blues Harmonic

## Facility

In the SPS, eight-tone scales are named directly from the scale phrases used to form them. As such, naming the scales that we've demonstrated above involves using far fewer major terms than would be used naming them by contemporary convention. For five of the SPS eight-tone scales featured above—Augmented Major, Augmented Diminished, Minor Minor 2, Minor 2 Augmented, Minor Augmented—we have allowed respective nicknames: Augmented, Augmented 2, Minor 3, Locrian, and Locrian M2. However, this allowance is nothing more than a gesture of concession, so to speak—and it's designed to be "temporary." We do this to help the student ease into our new system without being overwhelmed with memorization. Once you've fully grasped the system, you will more than likely refer to all of the above eight-tone scales by their SPS names.

All in all, though, you don't need to get overly concerned about memorizing the names of all of the known scales in Western music. Any given musician, over the course of his or her lifetime, will ordinarily use only a handful of scales. Most professional musicians don't even use all of the existing scales. So, if you don't use them, don't worry too much about their names. The SPS is not designed to pressure anyone to know everything there is to know about scales; it is designed just to simplify and to standardize.

## Leftovers

Shown next are four contemporary eight-tone scales that are not included in the selection demonstrated in Chapter 7. The scale phrases employed in each scale are noted in parentheses. These scales, which employ Unusual scale phrases (introduced on page 36), are not frequently used in modern Western music.

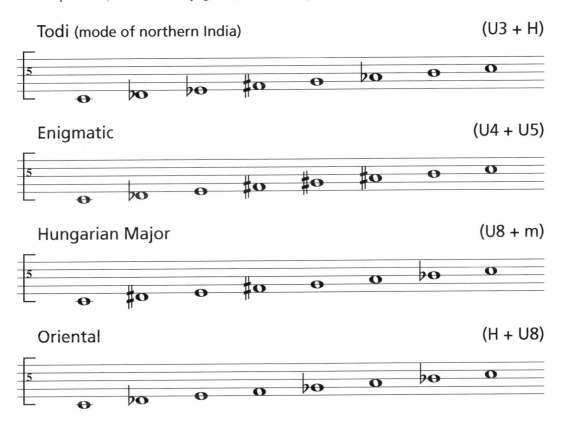

The Oriental Scale is the same as the mode built on the fifth scale degree of the Harmonic Scale. One contemporary name for this scale is Mixolydian ♭2 ♭5.

## Mode Names

Though the history of the modes is complex and lengthy, we offer an extremely abrigded account of the origination and development of the modes:

Around 400 CE, four modes were adopted by St. Ambrose: Dorian, Hypodorian, Phrygian, and Hypophrygian. Four more were later added sometime between 540 and 600 CE: Lydian, Hypolydian, Mixolydian, and Hypomixolydian. These modes, later labeled "church modes," were actually general modes used by all classes of musicians. Then, in 1547, Heinrich Glarean, a Swiss monk, introduced yet another four: Aeolian, Hypoaeolian, Ionian, and Hypoionian. Glarean also theoretically suggested the hyperaeolian (B3-B4) and the hyperphrygian (F3-F4); these two modes were later formally accepted and respectively renamed the Locrian and Hypolocrian, bringing the final mode count to fourteen. At some point early in the Baroque period (1600-1750), the modes prefixed "hypo" (then labelled "plagal") were discarded leaving only seven (then labelled "authentic"). Only two of the remaining seven, the Ionian and the Aeolian, remained in popular use; subsequently, they were formally accepted and established respectively as the Major and Minor Scales.

Listed below are the mode names that are used in this text. We refer to the seven modes built on the Major Scale (i.e., the seven former "authentic" modes) as the *Glarean Modes*. These modes are still ordinarily referred to by any one of several other names: Medievel, Church, Ecclesiastical, Gregorian, etc. Regarding these seven modes, however, the term "Glarean" is more accurate than any of the other terms, and it is for the most part all-encompassing.

In this text, we refer to the seven modes built on the Minor Major Scale as the *Post-Glarean Modes*. To inauguarate a standard concordant with the historical Glarean modes, we have judiciously assigned Byzantine-derived names to these modes. Though Jazz students may choose to refer to these modal structures by their directly corresponding scale names, we encourage all students to incorporate these new names into their musical vocabulary. With this text, we believe that we have completed the organization and codification of all of the useful modes as previoiusly employed in Western music.

## Mode Names

| *Glarean* | *Post-Glarean* |
|---|---|
| Ionian | Mysian |
| Dorian | Pamphrylian |
| Phrygian | Galatian |
| Lydian | Lycian |
| Mixolydian | Bithynian |
| Aeolian | Carian |
| Locrian | Cilician |

# Chapter 9

# OTHER SCALES

Because of the many different systems of tempering, we could literally have thousands of different, individual tones; subsequently, we could have thousands of scales. Of the enormous number of possible scales, there are some contemporary scales that may be encountered by the student at some point in study or composition; in this chapter, we demonstrate some of those scales. For simplification and ease of memorization, some of those scales have been assigned new names. Some scales are included because they contain prominent scale phrases, and others are included because they further emphasize how interesting modes can be built on scales.

### Half Step (ascending)

### Half Step (descending)

This is the Half Step Scale. The contemporary name for this scale is Chromatic. There are thirteen tones in this scale (including the octave of the tonic). In this scale, all of the intervals between adjacent tones are half steps. The descending version of this scale may be notated using flat (♭) symbols instead of sharps.

### Whole Step

This is the Whole Step Scale. This scale contains four **augmented** scale phrases: Three are true, and one is *enharmonic* (i.e., notated differently but sounding the same); however, unlike those in an eight-tone scale, these scale phrases are *overlapping*, not adjacent.

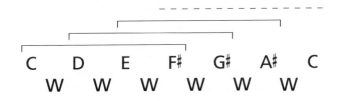

Contemporary names for this scale are Whole Tone and Auxiliary Augmented. You will recall that we try to avoid using the phrasal term "whole tone" in the names of scale phrases or scales. In an effort to maintain uniformity and consistency, we prefer the term "whole step" over "whole tone," and we reserve the use of the term "whole step" to mean just that—one whole step (two half steps). As this scale contains *only* whole step intervals between adjacent tones, we use the name Whole Step for this scale.

### Diminished (W)

This is the Diminished (W) Scale. This scale contains one true **diminished** scale phrase. The two other successively overlapping **diminished** scale phrases are *enharmonic*, not true.

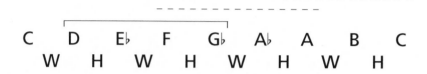

Contemporary names for this scale are Diminished, Diminished (Whole-Step), and Diminished Diminished. These names have been used by Jazz theorists because this scale is commonly used when improvising on Diminished chords and other select chords. The traditional name for this scale is Octatonic (with the octave of the tonic *not* included). This scale's intervals are ones *alternating* between whole and half steps. We have specifically named this scale Diminished (W) because of the prominent effect of the overlapping **diminished** scale phrases (regardless whether they are true or enharmonic), and because the first interval (the determinantal interval) in this scale is that of one whole step.

### Diminished (H)

This is the Diminished (H) Scale. This scale contains one true **diminished** scale phrase. The two other successively overlapping **diminished** scale phrases are *enharmonic*, not true.

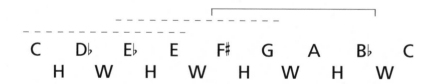

Contemporary names for this scale are Diminished (Half-Step), Dominant Diminished, Inverted Diminished, and Auxiliary Diminished. Jazz musicians might use this scale when improvising on Dominant 7th chords and other select chords. This scale's intervals are ones *alternating* between half steps and whole steps. We have specifically named this scale Diminished (H) because of the prominent effect of the overlapping **diminished** scale phrases (regardless whether they are true or enharmonic), and because the first interval (the determinantal interval) in this scale is that of one half step. The traditional names for this scale are Octatonic Variant and Symmetrical (now obsolete).

## Harmonic Overlap

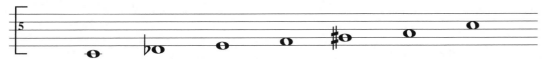

This is the Harmonic Overlap Scale. This scale contains two **harmonic** scale phrases; however, unlike those in an eight-tone scale, these scale phrases are *overlapping*, not adjacent.

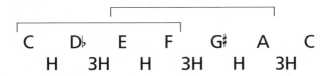

The contemporary name for this scale is Augmented Inverse, a scale which is a variation of the contemporary Augmented Scale. Of those two contemporary scales, the Augmented Inverse is the more sensible of the two contemporary scales. As such, we have deemed this scale worthy of inclusion in our study; however, because of its prominent overlapping **harmonic** scale phrases, we feel that the name of choice for this scale is Harmonic Overlap.

In the contemporary Augmented scale, the term "augmented" suggests that each three-half-step interval in that scale is that of an *augmented 2nd*, which, under ordinary circumstances, would be correct. However, if you construct the Augmented scale in a consistent "tone-to-tone" order, as you would with the Augmented Inverse (i.e., using *augmented 2nd* intervals *and* dropping the seventh scale degree), the scale would yield awkward and impractical notation: C, D♯, E, F✗ (F double sharp), G♯, A✗ (A double sharp), and C. Most notably, this sequence yields an interval at the end of this scale which proves to be that of a *doubly diminished 3rd*, an interval which is most uncommon. And to simply change those tones to enharmonic equivalents would make the whole procedure seem a bit arbitrary.

## Blues

We call this scale by its contemporary name—Blues Scale. The seven-tone version of this scale has an enharmonic **blues** scale phrase. This scale is popular with Blues and Jazz musicians.

The Blues Scale as demonstrated above is just one version of that scale, for the Blues Scale is certainly a flexible scale, and we say flexible for two reasons: (1) The tones chosen for inclusion in the Blues Scale are largely determined by the musician using the scale and by the particular style of the piece being played (Blues, Jazz, or related style). Some consider the Blues Scale (Minor Blues Scale) as a seven-tone scale (C, E♭, F, F♯, G, B♭, C), whereas others will include up to eleven tones (as suggested above); and (2) In the literal sense, depending on the instrument used to play the scale, the tones themselves can be considered flexible: they can be inflected (pitch bent). For example, horn players can play select tones slightly out of tune, or inflected. These select tones are referred to as *blue notes*. The tones of the scale most commonly chosen for inflection are the *3rd, 5th,* and *7th*. The pitches of the blue notes are not precisely fixed, so the resultant inflected pitches (the blue notes) lie somewhere between the *minor 3rd* and the *major 3rd*, between the *diminished 5th* and the *perfect 5th*, and between the *minor 7th* and *major 7th*.

## Six-Tone

This is the Six-Tone Scale. Contemporary names for this scale are Pentatonic, Major Pentatonic, and Mongolian. By SPS standards, the complete traditional Pentatonic Scale is actually a "hexatonic" (six-tone) scale (five tones plus the octave of the tonic). Shown below are the remaining modes of the Six-Tone Scale.

## Egyptian

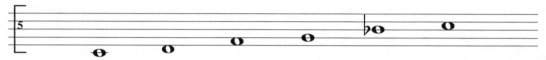

This is the Egyptian Scale. This scale is the same as the mode built on the second scale degree of the Six-Tone Scale.

## Ban Shiki Cho

This is the Ban Shiki Cho Scale. This scale is the same as the mode built on the third scale degree of the Six-Tone Scale.

## Ritusen

This is the Ritusen Scale. This scale is the same as the mode built on the fourth scale degree of the Six-Tone Scale.

## Minor Six-Tone

This is the Minor Six-Tone Scale. The traditional name for this scale is Minor Pentatonic. This scale is the same as the mode built on the fifth scale degree of the Six-Tone Scale.

Shown below are the Hira Joshi Scale and the four scales that are actually modes built on the Hira Joshi Scale.

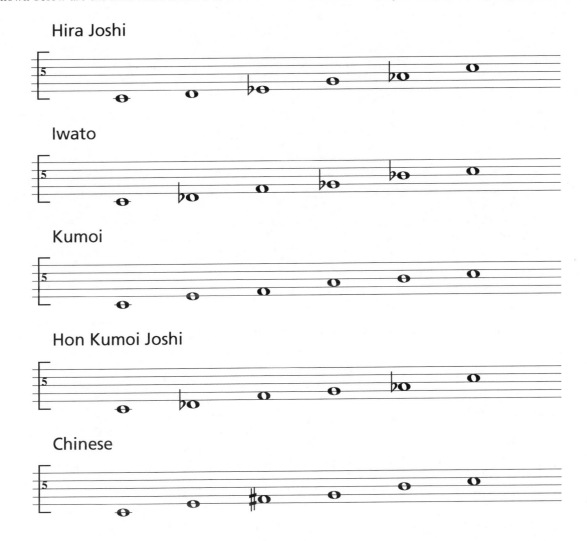

There are many interesting six-tone scales; listed here are a few of those scales (in the key of C): Kokin Joshi Scale (C, Dь, F, G, Bь, C); Scriabin Scale (C, Dь, E, G, A, C); Indian Scale (C, E, F, G, Bь, C); Balinese Pelog Scale (C, Dь, Eь, G, Aь, C); and Rwanda Pygmy Scale (C, D, Eь, G, Bь, C).

You might wish to further investigate scales. If you do, you need not be alarmed if you find that some of the scale names listed in this text are not identical to the scale names given in other texts. Many of the non-SPS scales have many alternate names. As the scope of this text was not meant to include a comprehensive demonstration of all possible scales, we have used scale names that are, for the most part, generally recognized.

## A New Perspective

Before we present our demonstration song and subsequently leave this section of the book, we'd like to briefly review what to this point has been our humble offering of a new perspective. Our purpose in presenting these new ideas is not to berate the long-standing traditional or contemporary methods. Our focus is primarily on that of simplifying and standardizing. We felt strongly that though the musical community could roughly make ends meet, it really didn't have a scale construction, identification, and classification system that genuinely brought consensus. So, to try to devise a scale construction and classification system that might be simple, synthetic, and satisfying, we had to enlist the services of the gentleman we refer to as "the foreigner." Granted, he's imaginary, but he proved to be exceedingly useful.

We imagined a man who lived in a land that had no music—*no* music whatsoever. We wondered what would happen if he came here and was introduced to music—but only aurally. That's right: he could *hear* any music that he wished to hear, but never be permitted to see notated music and never be permitted to study the history of music. After giving him a reasonable amount of time to get familiar with most genres of music, we would put him to the test: (1) He must find structural patterns in that music; (2) He must find a way to organize most of what he had heard; and (3) He must devise simple systems to relate to others what he had learned.

The SPS, then, is one of the systems that the foreigner devised. Once he discovered that the tones that we use are virtually always those of the Equal Temperament system (pages 8 and 85), his work was half done. That is, he quickly realized that in modern music, we use only so many tones; consequently, there can be only so many sensible eight-tone scales. Clinging to the old perspective does not alter the fact that time and again, we ultimately prefer and eventually use certain scales. In that light, we can take the SPS scales "as they are"; the fact that the contemporary scales (and their names) are historically based or harmonically based doesn't carry the weight that it once did.

As it stands today, the contemporary system (if you could even call it that) is in absolutely dreadful condition. Though that pseudo-system may have started out as one based on harmony, it inherently leads to the mixing of two theoretical schools of thought—the *modal* approach (with established intervals) and the *tonal* approach (with modified intervals). And as each year passes, with modification upon modification, the old system just gets more and more ridiculous: Lydian Major, Lydian Dominant, Major Locrian, Double Harmonic Minor, Hungarian Gypsy, and so forth. In texts outside of this book, contemporary scales are nothing more than "foster scales," passed from one home to the next, many of them being renamed every decade or so. Well, it doesn't have to be that way anymore. The SPS is an actual system—synthetic and independent—that provides a permanent and long-overdue home for scales, a home with a strong and practical foundation.

Looking at the SPS from the outside, the new student might initially find the system to be peculiar or a bit difficult to understand; however, once inside—once intimately tuned into the system—the student will discover how simple and logical the scales are and realize how easily these scales are formed and memorized. Essentially, all you really have, in any given application, are two simple scales phrases (some of which were once called *tetrachords*) combined to make one scale. And to keep matters simple, the scale thus formed is named after the scale phrases used to build the scale. It's not all that complicated. So, if you are a new student or are new to music theory, don't be discouraged. With due diligence and thought, the system will click for you. And once the scales are memorized, once the recalling and playing of any of the scales becomes second nature, the system itself won't even matter, for once you've found the treasure, the map is of no value.

# Chapter 10

# THE SCALE PHRASE IN PRACTICE

So far in this text, the scale phrase has been presented largely in theory. Now we will show how the scale phrase can work in practice. In our demonstration song, *Scale Phrase Ways*, each of the eight primary scale phrases is demonstrated at least once. In each measure, between the upper and lower staves, a symbol is used to identify the scale phrase notated directly above that symbol.

The scale phrases are identified as follows: M = Major; m = Minor; m2 = Minor 2; + = Augmented; O = diminished; H = Harmonic; A = Altered; and B = Blues. These symbols are "once-and-done" symbols used for instructional purposes only. Though similar to the symbols used in *System 2000 Chord Notation,* they are not the same.

Each chord used in *Scale Phrase Ways* is numbered. The number appears directly below each chord of the lower stave. The System 2000 chord symbols that correspond to those numbers are shown on page 64 and again on page 92. After you've finished studying System 2000, you may wish to come back to this song and write in the System 2000 chord symbols. Doing so will help you associate the chord symbols with the actual notation of the chords.

*Scale Phrase Ways* is a simple song with few embellishments. It is designed to help you become familiar with the scale phrases as they exist not just in theory but in practice. The scale phrases demonstrated in this song are shown in ascending and descending order. We hope that as you study and play this song, you will realize some of the useful attributes of the scale phrase.

The scale phrase is an excellent tool with which to learn the eight-tone scales. The scale phrases are quickly and easily learned, and once they are learned, you can simply combine them to form any eight-tone scale. Also, in the reverse sense, you can quickly and easily determine any eight-tone scale by identifying its scale phrases. All in all, if you become thoroughly familiar with the scale phrases—with their intervallic structures and the fingerings used to play them—you will become markedly adept at using any eight-tone scale. Also, the scale phrase can be very useful in the formation and development of melodic line. This four-tone structure can be especially useful for the new composition student who does not rely largely on intuition.

If you are a new student with limited faculty at the piano keyboard, simply play the tones of the upper stave of the system (with the right hand). Though they certainly provide a sense of fulfillment, the accompanying chords do not have to be played, for we are concerned more with the role of the scale phrase than we are with the song as a whole.

OK, let's check out the scale phrase way—with *Scale Phrase Ways*!

# Scale Phrase Ways

Joseph L. D'Agostino

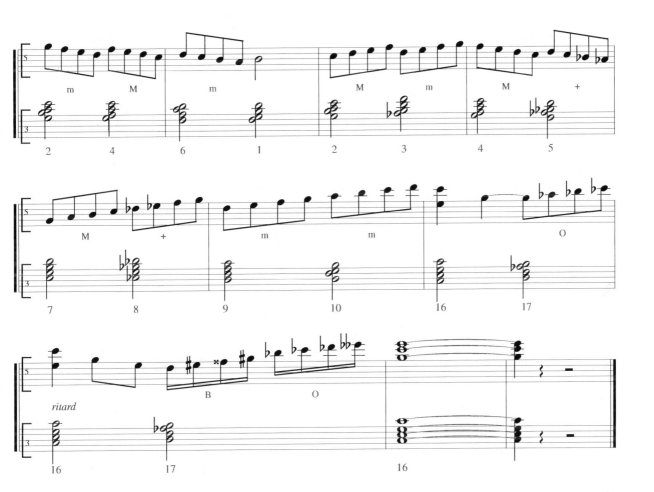

Shown below are the System 2000 chord symbols for *Scale Phrase Ways*.

| Chord #: | 1 | 2 | 3 | 4 | 5 | 6 |
|---|---|---|---|---|---|---|
| Notation: | $\dfrac{G^d_7}{F}$ | $\dfrac{C^M_7}{G}$ | $\dfrac{B^o_7}{A\flat}$ | $\dfrac{A^m_7}{G}$ | $\dfrac{B\flat^d_7}{F}$ | $\dfrac{D^m_7}{F}$ |

| Chord #: | 7 | 8 | 9 | 10 | 11 | 12 |
|---|---|---|---|---|---|---|
| Notation: | $E^m_7$ | $E\flat^d_7$ | $D^m_7$ | $\dfrac{G^d_7}{D}$ | $\dfrac{F^M_7}{E}$ | $\dfrac{B\flat^M_7}{F}$ |

| Chord #: | 13 | 14 | 15 | 16 | 17 |
|---|---|---|---|---|---|
| Notation: | $\dfrac{A\flat^M_7}{E\flat}$ | $\dfrac{A^m_7}{E}$ | $D^d_7$ | $C^M$ | $\dfrac{B^o_7}{D}$ |

## Prime Scales

Up to this point, we have seen that the formulation of an enormous number of scales is possible. Even so, the contemporary musician will ordinarily use only a few of those possible scales. Furthermore, when choosing a scale, the musician will seriously consider a particular scale's potential not only as a melodic resource but also as a harmonic resource; that is, he or she will determine whether or not useful major and minor triads can be built from the tones that comprise that particular scale.

In that light, some modern theorists recognize a unique set of five scales, a set that they refer to as *prime scales*. The contemporary names for those five scales are Major, Melodic Minor, Harmonic Major, Harmonic Minor, and Double Harmonic Major. From three of these five scales, three other prime scales can be derived— as modes, that is; and those three mode-scales are the scales that are named Natural Minor, Melodic Major, and Double Harmonic Minor. The Natural Minor Scale is actually the Aeolian mode of the Major Scale; the Melodic Major Scale is actually the Mixolydian mode of the Melodic Minor Scale; and the Double Harmonic Minor Scale is actually the Lydian mode of the Double Harmonic Major Scale.

To qualify as a prime scale, every tone in a given prime scale must be a member of at least one major triad or one minor triad. (Triads are discussed on page 74.) Additionally, a given scale *cannot* contain a disqualifying succession of half-step intervals between tones; that is, in the case of the scales named Major, Natural Minor, Melodic Minor, Melodic Major, Harmonic Major, and Harmonic Minor, there cannot exist *two* half-step intervals in succession; and, in the case of the scales named Double Harmonic Major and Double Harmonic Minor, there cannot exist *three* half-step intervals in succession.

The designation of prime scales is a useful one, for the composer will readily know which scales are uniquely structured for facilitating optimal melodic and harmonic benefit.

For the eight (five plus three) prime scales, the contemporary/SPS names are as follows: Major/Major; Natural Minor/Minor 3; Melodic Minor/Minor Major; Melodic Major/Major Minor 2; Harmonic Major/Major Harmonic; Harmonic Minor/Minor Harmonic; Double Harmonic Major/Harmonic; and Double Harmonic Minor/Altered Harmonic.

# System 2000 Chord Notation

## Chapter 11

## THE SYSTEM 2000 CHORD SYMBOL

A systematic collection of chord symbols is a language. If we want to notate a given chord such that someone else can play that exact chord, we can place notes on a stave, or we can use an alternate graphic form—a *chord symbol*. In certain notational formats, those in which space constraints must be considered, using actual notes written on staves to supply a substantial number of chords can prove to be cumbersome. Instead, we can use chord symbols. Then, we can be almost certain that any musician interpreting our chord symbols will play the exact intended chords. Right? Well, maybe.

In music notation, few other methods are as controversial as those of chord symbol notation. Jazz and Popular music reigned in the twentieth century, and yet even though Jazz has been around for over eighty years and Popular music for over one hundred years, there isn't mutual agreement on the method of chord notation. Surprisingly, we haven't had a practical, standardized, universally accepted system. Until today.

System 2000 will at last bring harmony to the practice of chord symbol notation. We will discover that System 2000 will be assimilated into our musical repertoire quickly and easily; that System 2000 will be sensible and practical; and that System 2000 will improve communication between modern musicians.

System 2000 will accomplish this task by meeting the requirements of a good chord notation system. Those requirements are as follows:

1) The system must provide for positive **on-sight** identification of the chord. Identification must be **quick** and **easy**.
2) The chord notation itself must take up **minimal space** on the score. The notation should demonstrate the chord's structure and qualities utilizing no more than **two** adjacent vertical line spaces and no more than **seven** adjacent horizontal character spaces.
3) The system must use **symbols** that are generally understood, ones having respective meanings that are not vague. All included symbols must be those that are easily learned and retained.
4) The system should be one which is **independent**, not one of a coalescence of two or more methods.

Let's take a look at how System 2000 meets these requirements.

To some musicians, our System 2000 chord symbol may slightly resemble those that have been used before and those that are presently being used, but there are differences that make the System 2000 symbol decidedly superior. Figure 11.1 shows an example System 2000 chord symbol.

figure 11.1

The System 2000 chord symbol is notated in a specific order; likewise, its *name* is spoken in a specific order: 1) Root Tone; 2) Type Indicator; 3) Size Indicator; 4) Modifiers. The chord symbol in figures 11.1 and 11.2 is spoken "C Major Seventh with a *diminished 5th*." The modifier—the *diminished 5th*—is clearly noted in both symbolic form and spoken order.

figure 11.2

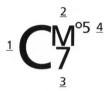

To clearly interpret and thoroughly understand our symbol, we must define in detail the names of the individual components, along with any related terms. Remember: As we mentioned in Chapter 4, we use *italics* to indicate *specific intervals* or *tones at specific intervals* (e.g., *5th, fifth*), and normal type to indicate *chords* (e.g., 5th, fifth).

## Base Chord

The *base chord* is the *root tone* combined with the *type indicator* and the *size indicator*. A base chord is a chord *without* modifiers. Figure 11.3 shows an example of a base chord.

figure 11.3

In System 2000, only twenty-two base chords are used. We will talk more about base chords in Chapter 12.

## Root Tone

The *root tone* is the base or foundation upon which the chord is built. It is the determining factor of the chord. The root tone is to the chord what the tonic is to the scale.

## Type Indicator

This symbol indicates the *type* of chord—Augmented, Major, Dominant, Minor, or Diminished. More specifically, this symbol indicates the type of chord *before modification* (if any). The order of the superposition of the *3rds* determines the *type* of chord. (We will demonstrate chord building in Chapter 12.)

The five chord types and corresponding symbols are as follows:

$$+ = \text{Augmented}$$
$$M = \text{Major}$$
$$m = \text{Minor}$$
$$d = \text{Dominant}$$
$$O = \text{Diminished}$$

In System 2000, these are the only chord types. To keep the number of symbols to an absolute minimum, only five symbols are used to indicate the chord type.

Now we'll take a detailed look at these symbols to see why they are being employed here.

"+"
This symbol, the plus sign, indicates that the base chord is an Augmented chord. System 2000 uses this symbol instead of "Aug" or "♯." This symbol has been employed by musicians for many years and seems to be one of the few things that Jazz and Pop musicians agree on.

"M"
This symbol, the capital "M," indicates that the base chord is a Major chord. System 2000 uses this symbol instead of "MA," "Ma," "Maj," "maj" or the delta/triangle sign. This symbol takes up little space, and it is easily and widely recognized as Major.

"m"
This symbol, the lowercase "m," indicates that the base chord is a Minor chord. The auxiliary symbol—the letter "m" with a line over it—is also used in System 2000. When chord symbols are not notated neatly, the "m" for "Minor" may be misinterpreted as the "M" for "Major." If you think there will be any chance of misinterpretation, use the auxiliary symbol. System 2000 uses these very economical symbols instead of "MI," "Mi," "min," "mi," or "-."

"d"
This symbol, the lowercase "d," indicates that the base chord is a Dominant chord. System 2000 uses this symbol instead of "Dom," "dom," "V," "X," or "x." We specifically use the lowercase "d" in System 2000 for one important reason: If we placed a capital "D" directly beside the letter representing the root tone, confusion could result over whether or not that capital "D" were representing a *tone*. Traditionally, when a Dominant chord is called for, the chord symbol is notated using only the root tone and a number: for example, "C7." In the past, this practice had sometimes caused confusion; and it still may cause confusion today, notably for new students. This confusion sometimes occurs because the use of the symbol "7"—without any other indicators or identifiers—does not definitively prompt the use of a *7th* at a specifically established interval. Seventh chords do indeed contain a *7th*, but the use of the lone "7," though common practice for many, may still be vague or confusing to others.

"O"
This symbol, a circle, indicates that the base chord is a Diminished chord. Like the symbol "+" for augmented, this is one of the few symbols used in chord notation that musicians agree on. System 2000 uses this symbol instead of "Dim," "dim," or "♭." Employing this symbol should not cause confusion.

Note: In light of how System 2000 makes every attempt to avoid the mixing of terms or practices from two or more different methods, we must clarify the inclusion and use of the traditional term "dominant" as it relates to the Dominant chord present in System 2000:

The *scale degree* name "dominant" is recognized in both traditional music theory *and* System 2000. The *chord name* "Dominant" is also recognized by both systems. Beyond those commonalities, though, there are notable differences in each system's motivations for the use of the term "Dominant" as it relates to chords. In traditional theory, the Dominant chord ordinarily assumes what can be referred to as a *dominant function*. That is, in chord progression, the Dominant chord—the chord built on the dominant scale degree—tends to resolve to (move back to) the tonic chord. This resolution affords a sense of closure, and as such, the Dominant chord is ranked second in importance to the tonic chord. In System 2000, the Dominant chord is a discrete chord, with its function determined solely by the composer—for whatever purpose or effect. In System 2000, though not obvious on the surface to some, the motivations for establishing the Dominant chord—with the crucially integral *minor 7th*—are clear and strong. To very rudimentarily explain the key motivational factor, we offer the following:

The *harmonic series* specifies the individual components of a *tone*, those components being the *fundamental* and its many *partials*. The 7th and 14th partials of any given tone are both a *minor 7th* above respective octaves of the fundamental tone (see figure 14.9, page 92). These partials, though scientifically determined, are ordinarily discerned by the listener—sort of intuitively, or subconsciously. As the effect of their presence (i.e., their dominance as specific *7ths*) in the harmonic series is too profound to be ignored, we include our System 2000 Dominant chord—replete with the *minor 7th*. The term "Dominant" is accepted into our system not as an exception but as a logical necessity. Its inclusion also keeps with one of this book's philosophies, that of keeping the introduction of new terms to an absolute minimum. Note: When referring to a *chord*, we use the word "Dominant" (uppercase "D"); when referring to a *scale degree*, we use the word "dominant" (lowercase "d").

## Size Indicator

This symbol (or lack thereof) indicates whether the chord is a 5th (fifth), a 7th (seventh), a 9th (ninth), an 11th (eleventh), or a 13th (thirteenth). No indicator is used to indicate 5th chords, so there are only *four size indicators*.

The *size indicators* are the numbers "7," "9," "11," and "13." If a 5th chord is called for, the space used for the size indicator is left blank.

The *name* of the base chord itself is taken from the size indicator. **The *size indicator* number indicates the highest tone in the base chord**. For example, the "C Major 7th" chord is named as such because the highest tone in that base chord is a "*7th*."

Figure 11.4 shows the chord symbol for a "C Major 5th" chord. Note that there is *no* size indicator for this chord.

figure 11.4

Figure 11.5 shows the chord symbol for a "C Augmented 7th" chord. The size indicator is used in this chord symbol.

figure 11.5

We need to point out one *excellent* feature of System 2000: the notation of the base chord. The placement of the type indicator and the size indicator makes it virtually impossible to get confused as to which chord you are dealing with. The vertical stacking of the indicators—clearly differentiated from the modifiers—makes this system superior to the other downright confusing systems presently being used.

**As notated with System 2000, the chord symbol is interpreted by *positive action*: It is virtually impossible to misinterpret the chord as a whole, or to misinterpret the individual tones of the chord.**

# Modifier

The *modifier*—a number or symbol/number combination—clearly indicates which modifications have been made to the base chord. The modifier clearly states *which interval* has been modified, and *what exact modification* has been made to that interval. The modifier can also indicate that a tone has been *added to* or *removed from* the base chord. There are many different symbols used as modifiers, but you may already be familiar and comfortable with most of them. Let's take a look at the modifiers used in System 2000.

# Numbers

Each number represents the tone at that specific interval (e.g., 3 = *3rd* ).

## "3"

In System 2000, we do *not* modify this tone. This tone is a crucial tone in a chord; it profoundly effects the mood or feel of the chord. This tone *may* be omitted from the chord, but the effect of the chord will be noticeably different.

## "5, 7, 9, 11, 13"

These are commonly modified chord tones.

## "5, 7, 9, 11"

These tones may be omitted from a base chord.

## "7, 9, 11, 13"

Any of these tones may be added to a base chord (if the respective tones are not already included in the base chord). If any of these tones *at a major interval* are added to a base chord, the number may be written without one of the modifier symbols shown below. If there is *any* chance of creating confusion, though, precede the number with a symbol.

## "2, 4, 6"

These chord tones are sometimes added to base chords. They may be modified, though ordinarily they are not. If any of these tones *at a major interval* are added to a base chord, the number may be written without one of the modifier symbols shown below. If any of these tones at an interval *other than a major interval* are to be added to the chord, the number must be preceded by an appropriate modifier symbol. One octave higher, the *2nd, 4th,* and *6th*, are respectively the *9th, 11th,* and *13th*; however, though technically they are respectively the same tones in letter name, the actual coloring of the sound of any given chord is considerably different with the use of the *2nd, 4th,* or *6th* than it is with the *9th, 11th,* or *13th*.

## "8, 10, 12"

These tones may be added to any base chord; however, their respective addition would essentially constitute a doubling of the *tonic, 3rd,* and *5th.* This doubling practice is common in scoring music for large ensembles, but it is not necessary or desirable in scoring music for small groups.

# Symbols

## "++"

This symbol is placed in front of a number to designate that the interval at that number is to be that of a *doubly augmented*. This symbol is included strictly for completeness, for it is not employed in this text.

## "+"

This symbol is placed in front of a number to designate that the interval at that number is to be that of an *augmented*. This symbol is easily recognized and commonly used.

"P"

This symbol is placed in front of a number to designate that the interval at that number is to be that of a *perfect*. This symbol is used only to prevent confusion when the interval of the *5th* is raised from the *diminished* position. As such, this symbol is rarely used.

"M"

This symbol is placed in front of a number to designate that the interval at that number is to be that of a *major*. As we mentioned earlier, this is a common symbol, easily recognized and widely used.

"m"

This symbol is placed in front of a number to designate that the interval at that number is to be that of a *minor*. This symbol is very economical and easily recognized. If there is any chance of misreading (just as in the case of the type indicator), use the auxiliary symbol—the letter "m" with a line over it.

"o"

This symbol, a small circle, is placed in front of a number to designate that the interval at that number is to be that of a *diminished*. As we mentioned before, this is a generally accepted symbol.

"oo"

This symbol, a combination of two small circles, is placed in front of a number to designate that the interval at that number is to be that of a *doubly diminished*. This rarely employed symbol is used only once in this text.

"n"

This symbol is placed in front of a number to indicate that the tone at that interval is *not* present in the chord. For example, the symbol "n5" would indicate that there is *no 5th* in the chord being modified.

Of the eight modifier symbols, *four* are frequently used: +, M, m, and o.

**Note: In System 2000, we reserve accidentals (e.g., ♯, ♭) for use with tone names (letters)—and for that use only.**

You may have noticed the conspicuous absence of two other symbols—the "minus sign" and the "parenthesis." We believe that these symbols generally cause confusion, so we have not considered them for use in System 2000.

Figure 11.6 shows a sample chord using modifiers. The chord is a "C Major 9th with a *diminished 5th*."

figure 11.6

Figure 11.7 shows another sample chord symbol. This chord symbol has two modifiers. This chord is a "C Major with an added *major 6th* and an added *major 9th*."

figure 11.7

The modifiers in figure 11.7 indicate two things: (1) The tone at the interval of a *major 6th* is to be added to the chord; and (2) The tone at the interval of a *major 9th* is to be added to the chord. Notice that the modifiers in figure 11.7 are listed with the "9" above the "6." In the System 2000 chord symbol, the modified tones of the chord are ordered as they would be notated on a musical stave, with the highest numbered (pitched) tones on the top, and the lowest numbered (pitched) tones on the bottom.

## Slash

The slash (shown in figures 11.9, 11.10, and 11.11) is used to separate the base chord and its modifiers from the bass tone, if such a designation is called for.

## Bass Tone

The *bass tone* is the lowest tone of the chord structure. The root tone of any given chord structure does not have to be the lowest tone. Any member of the base chord or modified chord may be used as the lowest tone.

## Order

You can see that the System 2000 chord symbol is notated in an orderly manner. To make interpretation of the symbol perfectly clear, each of the components of the symbol has its specific designation and proper place in the symbol. Figure 11.8 shows the notated *position* of the components of an example System 2000 chord symbol. The lines (cap, mean, base), ordinarily invisible, are shown to clarify the position of the components.

figure 11.8

Referring to figure 11.8, we see that the *root tone*, the uppercase "C," is written on the base line. The letter's height extends from the base line to the cap line. Essentially, the letter is notated just as an uppercase letter would be notated.

The *type indicator*, the small capital "M," is written on the mean line and extends to the cap line.

The *size indicator*, the number "7," is written on the base line and extends to the mean line. Essentially, regarding this number's size, it is notated just as a small capital letter would be notated. When handwriting a chord, leaving a slight space between the type indicator and the size indicator will facilitate easier reading.

The *modifier*, the symbol/number combination "°5," is notated in superscript position directly to the right of the type and size indicators. The modifier is notated in a smaller size than that of the type or size indicator. Though the requirements for good chord notation prescribe that the chord symbol be notated within the confines of two adjacent vertical line spaces, notating the modifier in the superscript position is perfectly acceptable, for the superscript space, in this application, is essentially the same as the *ascender space,* the uppermost area of the vertical line space.

If the bass tone of the chord is a tone *other than the root tone*, a slightly different chord symbol is used. Figure 11.9 shows the properly notated symbol for a chord whose bass tone is *not* the root tone but the *3rd* of that chord.

figure 11.9

The symbol in figure 11.9 denotes a "C Minor 7th chord with an E♭ bass tone." This symbol demonstrates that properly notating such a chord involves using a horizontal slash with the base tone notated below it. Though this does involve using two adjacent vertical line spaces, this arrangement still satisfies the requirements of good chord notation.

Another way to notate this chord symbol would be to use the slash in the forward (diagonal) position. Figure 11.10 shows notation using the slash in that manner.

figure 11.10

Only in extreme cases will the notation of the chord require the use of the seven adjacent horizontal character spaces allowed in System 2000. Figure 11.11 shows the notation of an unusually "lengthy" chord: A♭ Augmented 9th with a *minor 7th* and with a G♭ bass tone. When notating by hand a chord such as this one, you will most likely (naturally, that is) use *proportional* spacing, which will tighten the chord symbol. As such, the chord symbol will probably take up less than seven full adjacent horizontal character spaces. For those musicians who use professional music notation software or page-layout software, System 2000 fonts will provide for simple and concise notation of chords.

figure 11.11

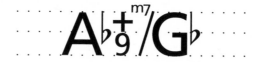

Now that we have thoroughly explained the System 2000 chord symbol, let's move ahead and take a look at some established, generally accepted chords, chords that in System 2000 are referred to as *base chords*.

# Chapter 12

# BASE CHORDS

The chords demonstrated in this text are not new chords. Most of the chords demonstrated are those familiar to many; most of them have been used for decades, some for centuries. System 2000 simply shows chords from a different perspective—at face value—and then goes on to provide a system of notation that is simple to use and easy to remember.

To make the process of learning and interpreting System 2000 chord symbols as simple as possible, we use what we call a *base chord*—a simplified, commonly accepted chord structure, to which modifications, if needed, may be made. Again, these base chords are ordinary, existing chords, common to most musicians. We use the base chord because it is beneficial to all musicians to have an established basic structure to work from. Base chords may be effectively used *with* or *without* modifications. The base chords demonstrated in this chapter are the 5ths, the 7ths, and the 9ths. We will show you features characteristic of each of the types and sizes of chords.

Before we look at the specific System 2000 base chords, let's first take a brief look at the structure simply and conventionally known as the *chord*. Though the focus of this book is on chord notation and not on specific harmonic properties or functions of the chord, a quick look at the conventional chord structure will help familiarize the new student with this important musical element.

## Chord
The chord is the product of three or more different tones sounding simultaneously or functioning as if sounded simultaneously.

## Chord Tones
The *root tone* is the tone that the chord is built on, and it is the tone from which the chord takes its name. If the root tone is the lowest tone of the chord, the chord is said to be in the "root position." Most of the chords in this text are shown in root position.

The *3rd* is the tone that is an interval of a *3rd* above the root tone. In System 2000, the *3rd* will be *major* or *minor*.

The *5th* is the tone that is an interval of a *5th* above the root tone. In System 2000, the *5th* will be *augmented*, *perfect*, *diminished*, *or* (rarely) *doubly diminished*.

The *7th* is the tone that is an interval of a *7th* above the root tone. In System 2000, the *7th* will be *major*, *minor*, or *diminished*.

The *9th* is the tone that is an interval of a *9th* above the root tone. In System 2000, the *9th* will be *augmented*, *major*, *minor*, or *diminished*.

**Note: the rules for the modification of intervals of a *chord* are the same as the rules for the modification of intervals of the *scale*.** Just as with the intervals of tones in a scale, the intervals of tones in any chord may be modified—within reason, that is.

## Construction of Chords

Chords are built with *3rds* that are superposed.* The order of the *3rds* determines the *type* of chord. The *3rds* used in construction of chords are "*major*" and/or "*minor.*" Figure 12.1 shows an example—the "C Major 9th" chord. This chord contains superposed *3rds*: (from lowest to highest) a *major 3rd*, a *minor 3rd*, a *major 3rd*, and a *minor 3rd*.

figure 12.1

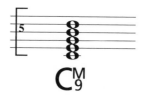

## Chord Name

As we mentioned in Chapter 11, the chord is named from the *highest* tone used in the base chord. If the highest tone in the base chord is a *5th*, the chord is called a "5th chord"; if the highest tone in the base chord is a *7th*, the chord is called a "7th chord"; and so on. In the above figure 12.1, the chord is named "C Major 9th" because the highest tone in the base chord is a *9th*. The size indicator "9" designates this property.

## 5th Base Chords

There are *four* 5th base chords. You may already be familiar with these as these are very simple and common chords. The 5th base chords used in System 2000 are shown in figure 12.2.

figure 12.2

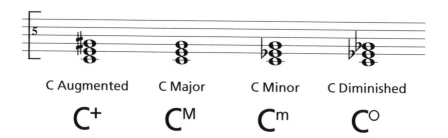

The 5th base chord contains a *root tone*, a *3rd*, and a *5th*.

This most basic and simplest chord—made with *three* tones—is conventionally and traditionally referred to as a "triad." Our System 2000 5th chord is indeed a triad (it has the *root tone*, *3rd*, and *5th*); however, in the ongoing effort to simplify and standardize chord notation and nomenclature, we much prefer to visualize this chord as a 5th chord. When speaking the name of this basic chord, though, you do not need to verbalize the term "5th" because in System 2000, the 5th is the default chord. Remember: If a System 2000 chord symbol has *no* size indicator, you know that the chord is a 5th chord.

* We use the term "superposed" (placed *above*) because true "superimposition" (placing *on top of*) of intervals would yield duplicate, unison tones. For example, in figure 12.1, the tones E, G, and B would be duplicated if the *3rds* were literally superimposed. Also, we do not refer to the intervals of *3rds* as being "stacked," as some do, because piano tuners use that term, and only when referring to three or more contiguous intervals; and we do not refer to the respective tones of a given chord as being "stacked" because that term semantically hints a sense of randomness not only in the choice of tones but in the specific order of those tones.

## 7th Base Chords

There are *five* 7th base chords. They are shown in figure 12.3.

figure 12.3

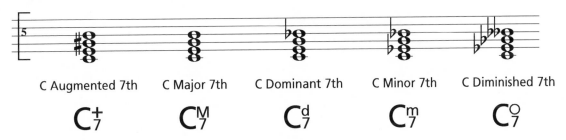

The 7th base chord contains a *root tone*, a *3rd*, a *5th*, and a *7th*.

## 9th Base Chords

There are *five* 9th base chords. They are shown in figure 12.4.

figure 12.4

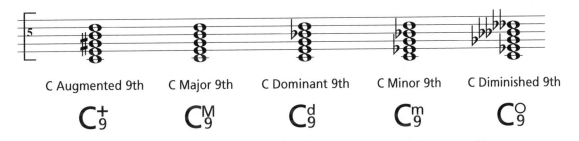

The 9th chord contains a *root tone*, a *3rd*, a *5th*, a *7th*, and a *9th*. The 9th chord, though not used as often as the 7th, is a popular chord and is commonly found in modern music.

In Chapter 13, we will discuss the many modifications that can be made to the 5th, 7th, and 9th chords.

11th and 13th chords, popular with twentieth-century Jazz musicians and Classical composers, will be demonstrated and discussed in Chapter 14.

## Inversion

Most of the chords in this text are shown in root position. Chords, however, can and do commonly occur in "inverted" positions. Figure 12.5 shows the "C Major" chord in its root and inverted positions.

figure 12.5

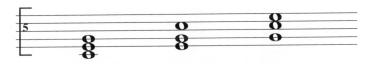

Root position    1st inversion    2nd inversion

The following chart shows the vertical order of the *3rds* as they occur in the 5th, 7th, and 9th base chords.

| Augmented 5th | Augmented 7th | Augmented 9th |
| --- | --- | --- |
|  |  | m |
|  | m | m |
| M | M | M |
| M | M | M |
| **Major 5th** | **Major 7th** | **Major 9th** |
|  |  | m |
|  | M | M |
| m | m | m |
| M | M | M |
|  | **Dominant 7th** | **Dominant 9th** |
|  |  | M |
|  | m | m |
|  | m | m |
|  | M | M |
| **Minor 5th** | **Minor 7th** | **Minor 9th** |
|  |  | M |
|  | m | m |
| M | M | M |
| m | m | m |
| **Diminished 5th** | **Diminished 7th** | **Diminished 9th** |
|  |  | m |
|  | m | m |
| m | m | m |
| m | m | m |

# Warning!

Before we continue our discussion of chords, we need to make a profound point—to some, an irritating point:

In the study of harmony, from the traditional standpoint, chords are generally regarded as vertical by-products of voice-leading (in which the sounding of tones from different lines of music occurs simultaneously). Many music scholars and theorists would shudder to think otherwise; and sure, without some sense of vertical harmonic structure, most compositions would probably sound frightening. However, as you'll observe in the next chapter, we take the chord at face value: What you see is what you get!

In defense of that position, we need to state two things: (1) By far, the use of the chord in modern music is liberal. Whether or not this practice is in everyone's best interest is uncertain, but it *is* nevertheless the case; and (2) Considering the multitude of inadequate systems being used to notate chords, the best way to set a lasting, mechanically sound standard is to begin with the chord, plainly and simply *as is*.

Let's now move on to the many modified chords.

# Chapter 13

# MODIFIED CHORDS

System 2000 is very straightforward and simple. However, to maintain order and uniformity in this system, a few hard-and-fast rules must be observed. Those rules—and there are only a few—are noted in the text in **boldface**.

We also include commentary on some of the chords, on certain current chord notation practices, and on other related topics. The trained musician may find some of the comments, ideas, or attitudes somewhat abrasive at first, but very soon after utilizing System 2000, he or she will realize the beauty of the system and embrace it.

**Rule #1- Changes made to intervals of a System 2000 chord must be notated in a manner reflecting compliance to the rules of interval change (introduced and stressed in Chapter 4).**

We can not overemphasize Rule #1. In Chapter 11, we noted that we reserve accidentals (e.g., ♯, ♭) for use solely with tone names (letters, e.g., A, B, C). Outside of this text, however, this practice is *not* observed. In traditional music notation, the inappropriate use of accidentals—a very long-running practice—has caused and still causes confusion for many musicians. This practice is presently viewed as acceptable, yet it is in gross contradiction to the rules of interval changes.

Here is the case in point: We know from the rules of interval changes that if we took the interval of a ~~major~~ *perfect* 5th and raised the higher of the two tones of that interval one half step that we would then have an *augmented 5th*. It can be no other way; the rules are simple and direct. However, in scale and chord notation outside of this text, you will most often hear the *augmented 5th* referred to or seen notated as a "♯5" or "sharp 5." Likewise, you will likely see a *diminished 5th* notated as a "♭5" or "flat 5," a *minor 9th* notated as a "♭9" or "flat 9," and so on. In System 2000, we do not refer to augmented intervals as being "sharped," and we do not refer to diminished intervals as being "flatted." Though this sort of notation may be understood and accepted by trained musicians, it clearly has no place in any system that attempts to provide a device for simple and sensible notation and the accurate interpretation of that notation. As such, it will behoove the novice to avoid this practice—completely.

Our next rule is crucial, for all forms of modification to chords in System 2000 hinge on this rule.

**Rule #2- Modifications are made only after the *base chord* has been established. In other words, to make a specific, modified chord using System 2000, we must make it by *modifying a base chord*.**

## Modified 5ths

Figure 13.1 shows thirteen 5th chords with modifications.

figure 13.1

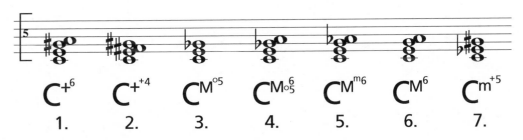

figure 13.1 cont.

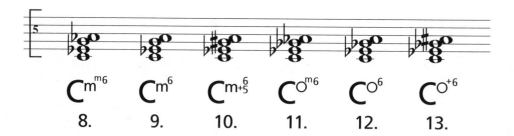

Chord #1 is a C Augmented with an added *major 6th*.
Chord #2 is a C Augmented with an added *augmented 4th*.
Chord #3 is a C Major with a *diminished 5th*.
Chord #4 is a C Major with a *diminished 5th* and an added *major 6th*.
Chord #5 is a C Major with an added *minor 6th*.
Chord #6 is a C Major with an added *major 6th*.
Chord #7 is a C Minor with an *augmented 5th*.
Chord #8 is a C Minor with an added *minor 6th*.
Chord #9 is a C Minor with an added *major 6th*.
Chord #10 is a C Minor with an *augmented 5th* and an added *major 6th*.
Chord #11 is a C Diminished with an added *minor 6th*.
Chord #12 is a C Diminished with an added *major 6th*.
Chord #13 is a C Diminished with an added *augmented 6th*.

## Commentary

Chord #12 is the *enharmonic equivalent* of the "C Diminished 7th" base chord. That is, they are notated differently but sound the same.

By contemporary standards, ten of the above chords—those with added *6ths*—might be viewed as "6th chords." In System 2000, we do not recognize a discrete 6th chord; to keep the system simple and concise, we view the *6th* as an "added tone." The added *6th* tone, if it is used, is ordinarily used with a Major or Minor chord. It is rarely, if ever, used with a Dominant chord.

**Rule #3- Of the five chord sizes in System 2000, the 5th chord is the *only* chord in which the highest tone of the base chord is allowed to be modified.** In the 7th, 9th, 11th, and 13th chords, the highest tone in each of those base chords is *not* allowed to be modified.

In System 2000, Rule #3 is very important: it provides a means for notating certain smaller, seldom-used chords such as numbers 3, 4, 7, and 10 in figure 13.1. Using traditional terminology, these odd chords—or any of the System 2000 modified chords—might be referred to as *altered chords* or *chromatically altered chords*. The contemporary musical term *chromatic* (from the Greek word *chroma*, meaning "color") implies that the chromatic tones provide a distinct and desired tone coloration.

System 2000 does indeed introduce what are referred to as *add-on* chords (explained below); however, the ten unusual chords in figure 13.1 that employ added *6ths* are simply referred to as "modified chords."

## Add-on 5ths

When a tone at an interval of a *3rd* or more above the highest tone in the base chord is *added to* a chord, that chord is referred to as an *add-on* chord. For example, Chord #2 in figure 13.2 shows an add-on chord—a "C Minor with an added *major 7th*." The added *7th* is an interval of a *3rd* above the highest tone of the base chord—the *5th*. In System 2000, add-on chords are necessary, for they provide a means to notate chords that otherwise would have to be notated in an awkward or confusing manner. Figure 13.2 shows four add-on 5th chords.

figure 13.2

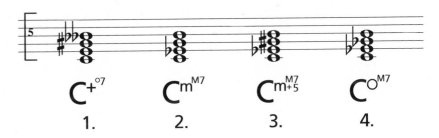

Chord #1 is a C Augmented with an added *diminished 7th*.
Chord #2 is a C Minor with an added *major 7th*.
Chord #3 is a C Minor with an *augmented 5th* and an added *major 7th*.
Chord #4 is a C Diminished with an added *major 7th*.

## Commentary

Chord #1 is the enharmonic equivalent of the "C Augmented with an added *major 6th*" chord (Chord #1 in figure 13.1).

To make other add-on 5th chords, you can add *minor* or *augmented 9ths* and/or *minor* or *augmented 11ths* and/or *minor* or *augmented 13ths* (see Add-on 7ths).

## Modified 7ths

Figure 13.3 shows eight 7th chords with modifications.

figure 13.3

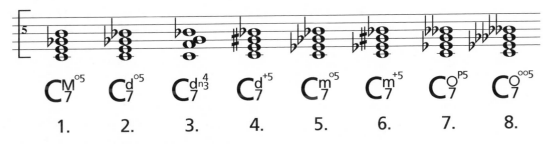

Chord #1 is a C Major 7th with a *diminished 5th*.
Chord #2 is a C Dominant 7th with a *diminished 5th*.
Chord #3 is a C Dominant 7th with an omitted *3rd* and an added ~~*major*~~ *perfect 4th*.
Chord #4 is a C Dominant 7th with an *augmented 5th*.
Chord #5 is a C Minor 7th with a *diminished 5th*.
Chord #6 is a C Minor 7th with an *augmented 5th*.
Chord #7 is a C Diminished 7th with a *perfect 5th*.
Chord #8 is a C Diminished 7th with a *doubly diminished 5th*.

## Commentary

Chord #5 is commonly referred to as a "C Minor 7 ♭5" or a "C Half-diminished," for which the contemporary symbol is often used; the contemporary symbol is a circle with a forward slash through it. As mentioned before, we do not refer to intervals as being "sharped" or "flatted." The so-called "Minor 7♭5" chord, in the literal sense, exists *only* as a 7th chord fashioned from either the SPS Locrian or Locrian M2 Scale. Still, even if it is fashioned from either of those scales, it can be derived from those scales *only* in *specific* keys—C, D, E, F, G, A, and B♭. Outside of those keys, there is no such thing as a "Minor 7♭5" chord.

Also, we do not use the contemporary symbol or the term "half-diminished," and we do not do so for three reasons: (1) To keep terms and symbols to an absolute minimum in System 2000, we purposely have not included the contemporary symbol. We are satisfied that the four frequently used System 2000 modifier symbols are adequate; (2) Though the term "half-diminished" may be clear to some, it is by design an ambiguous term. The common "C Diminished" chord (a 5th chord) contains a *minor 3rd* and a *diminished 5th*. In that chord, there are only *two* intervals above the root. *One-half* of those two, the *5th*, is *diminished*, yet that chord, oddly enough, is *not* commonly referred to as a *"half*-diminished." The common "C Minor 7th with a *diminished 5th*" (the so-called C Half-diminished chord) contains *three* intervals above the root—the *minor 3rd*, the *diminished 5th*, and the *minor 7th*. As such, when dealing with *three* elements, the term *half*-diminished seems out of place; and (3) If we use the term "half-diminished" to differentiate between two specific chords, the Diminished 7th and the so-called Half-diminished 7th, we are then encouraging the use of arbitrary terminology, a practice unwelcome in an orderly, consistent system of chord notation.

Chord #3 is a "C Dominant 7th with an omitted *3rd* and an added ~~major~~ *perfect 4th*." We highlight this chord because this chord is often, in conventional notation, referred to as a type of "suspension" chord, such as "C Dominant Sus" or "C Sus4" or "C7sus4." The conventional notation of this particular chord comes from the fact that in traditional theory, chords were viewed as vertical by-products of voice leading (mentioned at the end of Chapter 12). If this chord occurred in a voice leading situation, the *4th* in this chord would ordinarily "resolve," so to speak, downward to the *3rd*. In other words, in any given linear movement of notes, the tone following the *4th* would be predisposed to be a *3rd*. However, in System 2000, we do not use the term "suspended" or "suspension," and we do not use the corresponding symbols for or abbreviations of those terms. We do not for three reasons: (1) To keep terms to an absolute minimum, we exclude the term "suspension" and any related symbols. Again, the four frequently used System 2000 modifier symbols are adequate; (2) In modern music, there is no guarantee that the *4th* in any chord will resolve down to the *3rd*. Some musicians will intuitively hear that the *4th* pleads to resolve to the *3rd*, yet some will not hear it; and (3) The *4th* is *not* the only suspension tone. The *2nd*, *7th*, and *9th* are also traditional suspension tones. Considering the above, System 2000 treats the *4th* as an "added tone."

Regarding Chord #3, we also need to address another interesting facet of the practice of the omission of the *3rd* and the addition of the *4th*. The way to construct Chord #3 with only *one* step is simply to take the "C Dominant 7th" chord and *augment* the 3rd. We'd end up with a chord enharmonically equivalent to Chord #3. However handy and concise it may seem, that shortcut is not permissible in System 2000; and we mention this now in light of our fourth rule.

**Rule #4- In System 2000, we do *not* modify the *3rd*. The *3rd* is the second most significant tone in the base chord, and the effect of its modification in any base chord is too profound. The *3rd* may be omitted entirely; however, omitting the *3rd* must be done judiciously.**

Chord #3 does have the *3rd* omitted. *3rds* may be omitted, but their omission will ordinarily alter the effect of the chord. You may wish to experiment with certain chords to see whether or not the omission of the *3rd* provides the desired effect.

Chord #5 is the enharmonic equivalent of the "C Diminished with an added *augmented 6th*" chord (Chord #13 in figure 13.1).

Chord #7 is the enharmonic equivalent of the "C Minor with an added *major 6th*" chord (Chord #9 in figure 13.1).

Before we get into the larger chords, we will introduce Rule #5. We do so now because you will eventually notice that the *7th* is rarely omitted, and its position in the chord is commonly and conspicuously that of a *minor 7th* or a *major 7th*.

**Rule #5- In System 2000, the *augmented 7th* interval is not used.**

## Add-on 7ths
As there are a huge number of add-on possibilities with 7th chords, we will demonstrate only eight. Figure 13.4 shows eight add-on 7ths.

figure 13.4

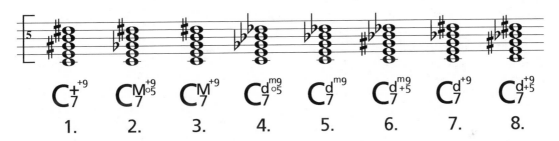

Chord #1 is a C Augmented 7th with an added *augmented 9th*.
Chord #2 is a C Major 7th with a *diminished 5th* and an added *augmented 9th*.
Chord #3 is a C Major 7th with an added *augmented 9th*.
Chord #4 is a C Dominant 7th with a *diminished 5th* and an added *minor 9th*.
Chord #5 is a C Dominant 7th with an added *minor 9th*.
Chord #6 is a C Dominant 7th with an *augmented 5th* and an added *minor 9th*.
Chord #7 is a C Dominant 7th with an added *augmented 9th*.
Chord #8 is a C Dominant 7th with an *augmented 5th* and an added *augmented 9th*.

To make other add-on chords using the 7th as the base chord (with no existing additions above the interval of the *7th*), you may simply add a *minor* or *augmented 9th* to any 7th base chord or modified 7th chord:

$$\textbf{7th}^{\text{mg}} \quad \text{or} \quad \textbf{7th}^{+9}$$

Or, you may add *minor* or *augmented 9ths* and *minor* or *augmented 11ths* in any of the following combinations:

| **11ths-** | m | + | m | + |
|---|---|---|---|---|
| **9ths-** | m | m | + | + |

Or, you may add *9ths* and *11ths* and *13ths* in any of the following combinations:

| 13ths- | m | m | m | m | + | + | + | + |
|--------|---|---|---|---|---|---|---|---|
| 11ths- | m | m | + | + | + | + | m | m |
| 9ths-  | m | + | + | m | + | m | m | + |

## Modified 9ths

Figure 13.5 shows a variety of 9th chords with modifications.

figure 13.5

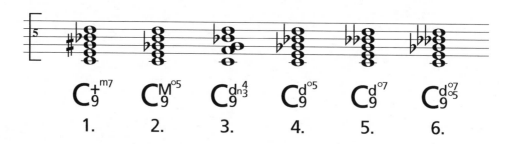

Chord #1 is a C Augmented 9th with a *minor 7th*.
Chord #2 is a C Major 9th with a *diminished 5th*.
Chord #3 is a C Dominant 9th with an omitted *3rd* and an added *~~major~~ perfect 4th*.
Chord #4 is a C Dominant 9th with a *diminished 5th*.
Chord #5 is a C Dominant 9th with a *diminished 7th*.
Chord #6 is a C Dominant 9th with a *diminished 5th* and a *diminished 7th*.

fig. 13.5 cont.

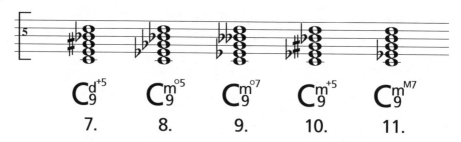

Chord #7 is a C Dominant 9th with an *augmented 5th*.
Chord #8 is a C Minor 9th with a *diminished 5th*.
Chord #9 is a C Minor 9th with a *diminished 7th*.
Chord #10 is a C Minor 9th with an *augmented 5th*.
Chord #11 is a C Minor 9th with a *major 7th*.

## Commentary

Chords #1 and #7, though named differently, are enharmonic equivalents. In System 2000, both notations are permissible. With System 2000, some chords may be notated in more than one way, yet interpretation of those chords will still be simple and clear.

In figure 13.6, Chord #9 is shown with an enharmonic equivalent, Chord #9a—a "C Minor with an added *major 6th* and an added *major 9th*."

figure 13.6

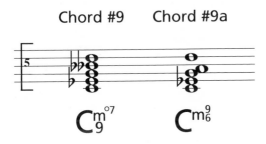

Both notations are acceptable in System 2000. Each of these chords, however, is realized in a different way. Making Chord #9a involves two movements: adding a *major 6th* and adding a *major 9th* to a "C Minor" base chord. For quite some time, this has been the conventional way of making that chord. Chord #9, the enharmonic equivalent of Chord 9a, is made in a simpler way. Making Chord #9 involves only *one* step: lowering by one half step the existing *minor 7th* of a "C Minor 9th" base chord.

Figure 13.7 demonstrates another example of how conservation of movement may be effected when making enharmonic equivalents. Chords A and B, both modified 5th chords, are enharmonic equivalents, and, like the examples above, are both realized differently. Making Chord A involves *two* steps: with a "C Major" base chord, lowering the *5th* one half step, and adding a *minor 6th*. Making Chord B (Chord #2 from figure 13.1) involves only *one* step: adding an *augmented 4th* to a "C Augmented" base chord.

figure 13.7

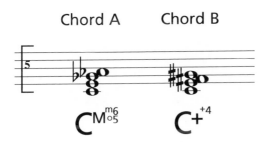

To some readers, the chords shown in figures 13.6 and 13.7 might seem to be a bit odd; however, they demonstrate the effectiveness of simple modification of base chords by select, minimal interval changes. In that light, we introduce our sixth and final System 2000 rule:

**Rule #6- When a base chord's interval is modified, the interval's movement from its home position in the base chord should be, whenever possible, that of only *one* half step.**

Figure 13.8 demonstrates the purpose of Rule #6. Shown are the "C Dominant 9th with a *diminished 7th*" (Chord #5, from figure 13.5), and the "C Major 9th with a *diminished 7th*" (Chord #5a).

figure 13.8

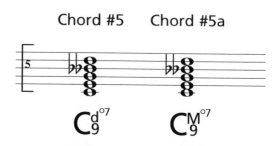

Though they are both actually the same chord, their names are indeed different, owing to the way in which they were formed. Chord #5a was formed by taking the "C Major 9th" base chord and lowering the *7th* one half step, and then lowering that *7th* one half step again—a total of *two* movements. Chord #5 was formed by taking the "C Dominant 9th" base chord and lowering the *7th* one half step—only *one* movement. In light of Rule #6, one name for this chord is preferred—"C Dominant 9th with a *diminished 7th*."

## Omission of 5ths

With chords numbered 5 and 9 (from figure 13.5), the *5th* could be omitted. Figure 13.9 shows the resultant chords.

figure 13.9

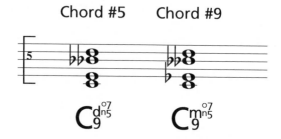

In 9th chords, as well as in 11ths and in 13ths, the *perfect 5th* is generally considered the least significant chord member, and it is sometimes omitted. This practice is common; however, when the *5th* is omitted from a chord (the harmonic element), it is generally included in the melody. Also, if the *5th* were omitted from a chord that is *of the same key* as that of the musical piece itself, and that chord were used to bring that piece to a conclusion, the perception of closure might be somewhat diminished. As with the *3rds*, you may wish to experiment with various omissions of *5ths* to obtain the desired musical effect.

## Add-on 9ths

There are many possibilities for add-on 9th chords. You may wish to experiment with the 9ths by adding various tones at intervals of *minor* or *augmented 11ths* and/or *minor* or *augmented 13ths*.

# Chapter 14

# OTHER CHORDS

Before we introduce the System 2000 11th and 13th chords, we will very briefly consider a few factors that affect the realization and characteristics of these "tall" chords.

As we mentioned in Chapter 2, our present system of temperament is called Equal Temperament (ET). Temperament denotes the arrangement of musical tones in which each tone will form a serviceable interval with any of the other tones. The ET tones are those that we are familiar with, those used by most musicians disciplined in Western music.

In Chapter 11, we mentioned the *harmonic series*. The harmonic series is an acoustic, underlying structure that our systems of tuning and tempering seem to mimic. The harmonic series comprises tones that are (acoustically speaking) pure tones. The ET tones, by mechanical necessity, are adjusted, or "tempered"; they are set at specific values. They are not exact matches of the pure tones; some are very close, but some are not. The ET tones are, so to speak, compromised pure tones (see figure 14.9, page 92).

Basically, then, what we are saying is this: It is virtually impossible to continue the superposing of *3rds* employing the intervals above the octave yet still maintain a harmonically perfect, or pure, structure. As long as we use ET tones and not tones closer to the tones of the harmonics series, we will not have a perfectly ordered chord (or scale) system. Due to the "unseen stiffness" imposed by ET, no single chord, acoustically speaking, will ring naturally pure. Regarding our 11th and 13th chords, we must be mindful that the pure tone that corresponds to the interval of the *11th* falls between the ET *major 11th* and the ET *augmented 11th*; that is specifically why in this text we refer to the ET tone at the interval of the *11th* as a *major* interval, and not a *perfect* interval, as some theorists would. Likewise, the pure tone that corresponds to the interval of the *13th* falls between the ET *minor 13th* and the ET *major 13th*.

All in all, though, ET has proven to be adequate, providing serviceable tones. The institution of ET seemingly hasn't hindered the use of 11th and 13th chords by musicians. By the end of the Romantic period of music, the 11th and 13th chords had become an established part of the harmonic vocabulary. And though the use of these chords seems to have peaked during the Impressionist period, contemporary Jazz musicians and serious modern composers still frequently employ these chords.

The *11th* is the tone that is an interval of an *11th* above the root tone; the *13th* is the tone that is an interval of a *13th* above the root tone. Though our focus here is on the 11th and 13th chords, we need to mention that both the *11th* and *13th* can work nicely, or colorfully, in the melody of a composition (with a 5th, 7th, or 9th chord accompaniment).

Let's now take a look at our 11th and 13th chords.

## 11th Base Chords

Figure 14.1 shows the four 11th base chords.

figure 14.1

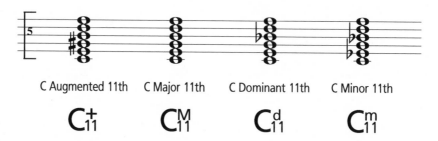

The 11th base chord contains a *root tone*, a *3rd*, a *5th*, a *7th*, a *9th*, and an *11th*. Of the five types of 11th chords, the Dominant 11th is the type that's most commonly used.

## 13th Base Chords

Figure 14.2 shows the four 13th base chords.

figure 14.2

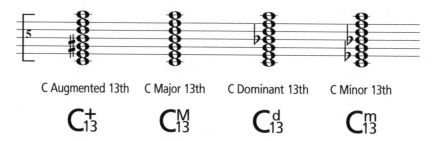

The 13th base chord contains a *root tone*, a *3rd*, a *5th*, a *7th*, a *9th*, an *11th*, and a *13th*. Of the five types of 13th chords, the Dominant 13th is the type that's most commonly used.

We include the Augmented 11th chord and the Augmented 13th chord because use of these base chords provides for simpler and neater chord notation. When making a desired chord with specifically chosen raised or lowered intervals, fewer modifiers will be required if the established base chords being used already contain those raised or lowered intervals.

The following chart shows the vertical order of the *3rds* as they occur in the 11th and 13th base chords.

| Augmented 11th | Augmented 13th |
|---|---|
|  | M |
| m | m |
| m | m |
| m | m |
| M | M |
| M | M |

| Major 11th | Major 13th |
|---|---|
|  | M |
| m | m |
| m | m |
| M | M |
| m | m |
| M | M |

| Dominant 11th | Dominant 13th |
|---|---|
|  | M |
| m | m |
| M | M |
| m | m |
| m | m |
| M | M |

| Minor 11th | Minor 13th |
|---|---|
|  | M |
| m | m |
| M | M |
| m | m |
| M | M |
| m | m |

You may have noticed that the construction of certain base chords yields contiguous intervals. All Augmented, Dominant, and Diminished base chords incorporate at least one contiguous interval; the Major 11th and 13th base chords each incorporate one. None of the Minor base chords incorporate contiguous intervals.

Now that we've established the 11th and 13th base chords, let's look at some modified versions of those chords.

## Modified 11ths

Figure 14.3 shows five Augmented 11th chords with modifications.

figure 14.3

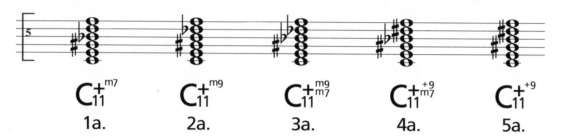

Chord #1a is a C Augmented 11th with a *minor 7th*.
Chord #2a is a C Augmented 11th with a *minor 9th*.
Chord #3a is a C Augmented 11th with a *minor 7th* and a *minor 9th*.
Chord #4a is a C Augmented 11th with a *minor 7th* and an *augmented 9th*.
Chord #5a is a C Augmented 11th with an *augmented 9th*.

Figure 14.4 shows five Major 11th chords with modifications.

figure 14.4

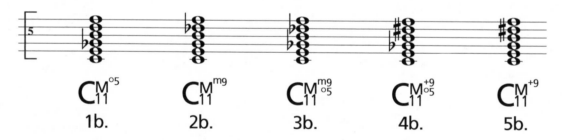

Chord #1b is a C Major 11th with a *diminished 5th*.
Chord #2b is a C Major 11th with a *minor 9th*.
Chord #3b is a C Major 11th with a *diminished 5th* and a *minor 9th*.
Chord #4b is a C Major 11th with a *diminished 5th* and an *augmented 9th*.
Chord #5b is a C Major 11th with an *augmented 9th*.

Figure 14.5 shows eight Dominant 11th chords with modifications.

figure 14.5

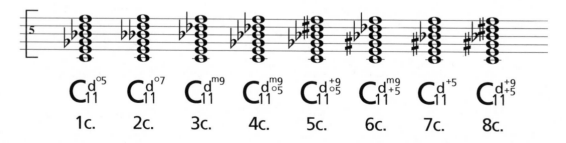

Chord #1c is a C Dominant 11th with a *diminished 5th*.
Chord #2c is a C Dominant 11th with a *diminished 7th*.
Chord #3c is a C Dominant 11th with a *minor 9th*.
Chord #4c is a C Dominant 11th with a *diminished 5th* and a *minor 9th*.
Chord #5c is a C Dominant 11th with a *diminished 5th* and an *augmented 9th*.
Chord #6c is a C Dominant 11th with an *augmented 5th* and a *minor 9th*.
Chord #7c is a C Dominant 11th with an *augmented 5th*.
Chord #8c is a C Dominant 11th with an *augmented 5th* and an *augmented 9th*.

Figure 14.6 shows seven Minor 11th chords with modifications.

figure 14.6

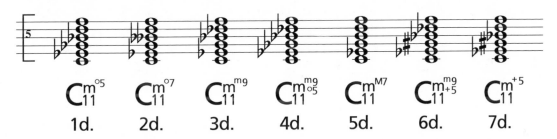

Chord #1d is a C Minor 11th with a *diminished 5th*.
Chord #2d is a C Minor 11th with a *diminished 7th*.
Chord #3d is a C Minor 11th with a *minor 9th*.
Chord #4d is a C Minor 11th with a *diminished 5th* and a *minor 9th*.
Chord #5d is a C Minor 11th with a *major 7th*.
Chord #6d is a C Minor 11th with an *augmented 5th* and a *minor 9th*.
Chord #7d is a C Minor 11th with an *augmented 5th*.

## Commentary

Chord #1a and Chord #7c, though named differently, are actually the same chord. Both notations are correct, and in System 2000, both notations are permissible.

Chord #3a and Chord #6c, though named differently, are actually the same chord. Both notations are correct, and in System 2000, both notations are permissible.

Chord #4a and Chord #8c, though named differently, are actually the same chord. Both notations are correct, and in System 2000, both notations are permissible.

As you experiment with large chords, you will discover that when *minor 9ths* are used simultaneously with *minor 3rds*, the effect may be perceived as being dissonant. (We briefly discuss dissonance in Chapter 15.)

If you investigate the music of twentieth-century composers, you might notice the following: In Minor 11th chords, tones are not ordinarily omitted; in large Dominant chords, *augmented 11ths* are not uncommon; and the *minor 9th/augmented 11th* combination is not uncommon.

## Add-on 11ths

To make an add-on 11th chord, you simply add a *minor* or *augmented 13th* to the 11th chord.

## Modified 13ths

Figure 14.7 shows several 13th chords with modifications.

figure 14.7

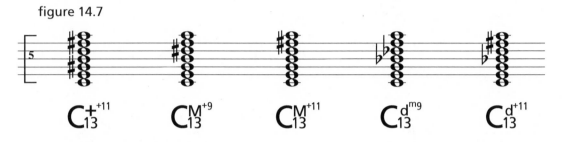

Chord #1 is a C Augmented 13th with an *augmented 11th*.
Chord #2 is a C Major 13th with an *augmented 9th*.
Chord #3 is a C Major 13th with an *augmented 11th*.
Chord #4 is a C Dominant 13th with a *minor 9th*.
Chord #5 is a C Dominant 13th with an *augmented 11th*.

## Commentary

If you investigate the music of twentieth-century composers, you might notice the following: In large Dominant chords, the *augmented 11th/major 13th* combination is not uncommon; in the Dominant 13th chord, sometimes both the *5th* and the *11th* will be omitted; and in Minor 13th chords, the *11ths* are ordinarily omitted.

The interval of the *minor 9th* is generally considered to be dissonant, so it must be used with discretion, if it is used at all.

The 11th and 13th chords are most effective in their respective root positions. When these chords are used in inverted positions, they lose some of their respective distinctiveness and are less effective at coloring a given composite sound. (We briefly discuss *tone color* in Chapter 15.)

A full Major 13th base chord contains seven tones. In a "C Major 13th" chord, for example, the tones included are C, E, G, B, D, F, and A. These tones are the same as those of the C Major Scale (less the octave of the tonic).

## Practicality

Now that we are familiar with System 2000, let's actually *use* it. Figure 14.8 shows four practice chords. We will analyze and notate them.

Remember: Before we can analyze any chord, we must vertically order the tones of the chord in *3rds* (see charts on pages 76 and 87). Having done that, we will have determined our root tone and will be ready to analyze the chord.

figure 14.8

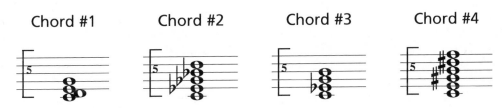

*Chord #1*
We see that the chord has a vertical order of *3rds* and that the root tone is a C: The chord is some form of "C" chord. The highest tone in this chord is a *5th*, so we know that this chord is a 5th chord. The *3rd* in this chord is a *major 3rd*, so we know that the base chord is a "C Major 5th." This chord also contains a *major 2nd*. Ultimately, the chord is a "C Major 5th with an added *major 2nd*." The chord would be notated as follows:

$$C^{M^2}$$

*Chord #2*
We see that the chord has a vertical order of *3rds* and that the root tone is a C: The chord is some form of "C" chord. We know that in System 2000, all of the 9th, 11th, and 13th base chords (except the infrequently used Diminished 9th base chord) contain a *major 9th*. This chord has the *major 9th*, a *9th* that has *not* been modified. This chord, then, is indeed a 9th, and not an add-on chord. As the *3rd* and *7th* are both *minor*, we know that the base chord is a "C Minor 9th." The *5th* is *diminished*, so, ultimately, the chord is a "C Minor 9th with a *diminished 5th*." The chord would be notated as follows:

$$C^{m^{o5}}_{9}$$

*Chord #3*
We see that the chord has a vertical order of *3rds* and that the root tone is a C: The chord is some form of "C" chord. Seeing that the highest tone in this chord is a *7th*, we would be tempted initially to think that this is some form of 7th chord; however, we quickly notice that the *3rd* in this chord is a *minor*. In the System 2000 7th chord, whether it be a base or modified 7th chord, if the *3rd* is *minor*, then the *7th* must be either *minor* or *diminished*. In this chord, it is not, so this chord can not be a 7th base chord or a modified 7th chord. It can only be a 5th chord—more specifically, an add-on 5th chord. We can plainly see, then, that we have a "C Minor 5th" base chord. With the inclusion of the *major 7th*, we ultimately have a "C Minor with an added *major 7th*." The chord would be notated as follows:

$$C^{m^{M7}}$$

*Chord #4*
We see that the chord has a vertical order of *3rds* and that the root tone is C: The chord is some form of "C" chord. We see that the highest tone is an *11th*, and that the *11th* is *not* modified. In the System 2000 11th base chord or modified 11th chord, the *11th* is always that of *major*. As such, our chord is indeed a "C 11th" of some type. The type, though, is easily determined, for the presence of the *major 3rd* and the *augmented 5th* show us clearly that the base chord is a "C Augmented 11th." Since the *9th* is modified—*augmented*—we have a "C Augmented 11th with an *augmented 9th*." The chord would be notated as follows:

$$C^{+^{+9}}_{11}$$

In this text, we have not shown *every* chord that can exist. We hope, though, that the assortment of chords that we have demonstrated will help you become comfortably familiar with these effectual structures. Practice does make perfect, so we highly recommend that you study any musical scores that you may have access to, especially scores of Classical music (e.g., those of Mozart, Ravel, Stravinsky). Eventually, you will realize that System 2000 provides the means to accurately analyze and neatly notate virtually any chord built in *3rds*—even those that look frightening. Using System 2000, you will be able to negotiate any chord with confidence.

Before we close this chapter, we again show the System 2000 chord symbols for the chords of the demonstration song in Chapter 10. After having read Chapters 11 through 14, you may now find these chords considerably less intimidating.

| Chord #: | 1 | 2 | 3 | 4 | 5 | 6 |
|---|---|---|---|---|---|---|
| Notation: | $\dfrac{G^d_7}{F}$ | $\dfrac{C^M_7}{G}$ | $\dfrac{B^O_7}{A\flat}$ | $\dfrac{A^m_7}{G}$ | $\dfrac{B\flat^d_7}{F}$ | $\dfrac{D^m_7}{F}$ |

| Chord #: | 7 | 8 | 9 | 10 | 11 | 12 |
|---|---|---|---|---|---|---|
| Notation: | $E^m_7$ | $E\flat^d_7$ | $D^m_7$ | $\dfrac{G^d_7}{D}$ | $\dfrac{F^M_7}{E}$ | $\dfrac{B\flat^M_7}{F}$ |

| Chord #: | 13 | 14 | 15 | 16 | 17 | |
|---|---|---|---|---|---|---|
| Notation: | $\dfrac{A\flat^M_7}{E\flat}$ | $\dfrac{A^m_7}{E}$ | $D^d_7$ | $C^M$ | $\dfrac{B^O_7}{D}$ | |

## Harmonic Series

Figure 14.9 shows notes that represent approximations of the first sixteen partials of the harmonic series of the fundamental tone C2 (65.4 Hz). The pitch of several of the pure tones deviates considerably from the ET tones that we are accustomed to hearing: the 7th partial is pitched lower than the B♭4 shown; the 11th partial is pitched lower than the F♯5 shown; the 13th partial is pitched higher than the A♭5 shown; and the 14th partial is pitched lower than the B♭5 shown.

figure 14.9

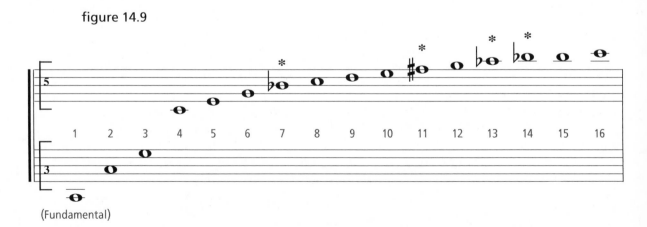

(Fundamental)

# Chapter 15

# COMBINATIONS

## Chords and Scales

We have shown quite a nice selection of chords, but if you are a new student, you may be wondering what to do with them. Well, the solution is simple: Mix a nice chord with a suitably sonorous scale—and you're off! The chart below lists eighteen SPS eight-tone scales, five non-eight-tone scales, and select chords that work reasonably well with those scales. Our combination list here is not comprehensive, but it should provide enough combinations to keep you busy for quite a while.

figure 15.1

| Scale | Chords |
|---|---|
| C Major | $C^{M}$  $C^{M6}$  $C^{M}_{7}$  $C^{M}_{9}$ |
| C Minor | $C^{m}$  $C^{m6}$  $C^{m}_{7}$  $C^{m}_{9}$  $C^{m}_{11}$  $C^{m}_{13}$ |
| C Minor 2 | $C^{m+5}$  $C^{m\,m6}$  $C^{m+5}_{7}$ |
| C Augmented | $C^{M}$  $C^{M\,o5}$  $C^{M\,o6_5}$  $C^{M6}$  $C^{M}_{7}$  $C^{M\,o5}_{7}$ |
| C Major Minor | $C^{d}_{7}$  $C^{d\,n3\,4}_{7}$  $C^{d}_{9}$  $C^{d}_{13}$ |
| C Minor 3 | $C^{d\,n3\,4}_{7}$  $C^{m}$  $C^{m+5}$  $C^{m\,m6}$  $C^{m}_{7}$  $C^{m+5}_{7}$  $C^{m}_{9}$  $C^{m}_{11}$ |
| C Locrian | $C^{m+5}$  $C^{m\,o5}_{7}$  $C^{m+5}_{7}$ |
| C Minor Major | $C^{m}$  $C^{m6}$  $C^{m\,M7}$ |
| C Minor 2 Minor | $C^{m}$  $C^{m6}$  $C^{m}_{7}$ |
| C Augmented 2 | $C^{+}$  $C^{+6}$  $C^{+}_{7}$  $C^{M\,o5}$  $C^{M\,o6_5}$  $C^{M\,o5}_{7}$ |
| C Augmented Minor | $C^{M\,o5}$  $C^{d\,o5}_{7}$ |
| C Major Minor 2 | $C^{+}$  $C^{d}_{7}$  $C^{d+5}_{7}$ |

figure 15.1 cont.

| | | | | | | | |
|---|---|---|---|---|---|---|---|
| C Locrian M2 | $C^{m+5}$ | $C_7^{m\,o5}$ | $C_7^{m+5}$ | | | | |
| C Dim. Augmented | $C^{m+5}$ | $C_7^{m\,o5}$ | $C_7^{m+5}$ | $C^{o}$ | | | |
| C Harmonic | $C^{M}$ | $C^{M\,m6}$ | | | | | |
| C Minor Harmonic | $C^{m}$ | $C^{m\,m6}$ | $C^{m\,M7}$ | | | | |
| C Major Harmonic | $C^{+}$ | $C_7^{+}$ | $C^{M}$ | $C^{M\,m6}$ | | | |
| C Harmonic Minor 2 | $C^{+}$ | $C^{M}$ | $C^{M\,m6}$ | $C_7^{d}$ | $C_7^{d\,n3\,4}$ | $C_7^{d+5}$ | $C_7^{d\,m9}$ |
| C Whole Step | $C^{+}$ | $C^{M\,o5}$ | $C_7^{d\,o5}$ | $C_7^{d+5}$ | $C_9^{d+5}$ | | |
| C Six-Tone | $C^{M}$ | $C^{M6}$ | $C_7^{M}$ | $C_7^{d}$ | $C_7^{d\,n3\,4}$ | $C_9^{d}$ | $C_{13}^{d}$ |
| C Minor Six-Tone | $C^{m}$ | $C^{m+5}$ | $C^{m\,m6}$ | $C^{m6}$ | $C_7^{m+5}$ | $C_9^{m}$ | $C_{11}^{m}$ $C_{13}^{m}$ |
| C Diminished (W) | $C^{o}$ | $C_7^{o}$ | | | | | |
| C Diminished (H) | $C_7^{d}$ | $C_7^{d\,o5}$ | $C_7^{m\,o5}$ | $C^{o}$ | $C_7^{o}$ | | |

# Compatibility

In music, the chord–scale relationship is prominent, powerful, and seemingly permanent. And as much as we like our SPS eight-tone scales just the way they are, we must admit that in modern music, scales are rarely used without some sort of harmonic support. A beautifully crafted chord will provide that support; and conversely, it will beckon a scale.

In that light, in figure 15.1, select chords were matched to each of the scales. Most of the combinations work very well. Depending on the listener, though, some combinations may not seem to sound as pleasant as others do. That is, when using certain scale/chord combinations, a sense of dissonance may be felt. As there really is no definitive, totally objective way to describe consonance or dissonance, we can very simply and generally say that certain combinations of tones sounded simultaneously are perceived to be consonant (pleasant or agreeable), and some are perceived to be dissonant (unpleasant or disagreeable).

Whether the effect of two or more tones sounded simultaneously is, or seems to be, consonant or dissonant depends largely on three factors: (1) the *timbre* (pronounced *tam*-ber) of the instrument(s) used to sound the tones; (2) the *octave* in which the tones are simultaneously sounded; and (3) the *listener*.

*Timbre*- Timbre, or "tone color," is the quality of a sound produced by an instrument (or voice). In relation to the fundamental, the number, strength, and duration of the integral harmonics determine the distinctive sound of a given instrument. Harmonics, then, determine why any given instrument sounds the way it does, and why two different instruments sound different than or similar to each other (e.g., the sound of the flute is distinctively different from that of the cello). Instrument design and the material used to construct the instrument profoundly affect how the tones are realized; those two factors determine the absence or presence of certain harmonics, consequently determining the quality of the sound generated by that particular instrument. Perceived consonance or dissonance is effected to varying degrees by the timbre of each respective instrument. For example, tone A sounded on instrument #1 may sound agreeable with tone B sounded on instrument #2, yet tone A may sound disagreeable with tone B as sounded on instrument #3.

*Octave*- When sounded in one octave, tones may be perceived differently than they are when sounded in another octave. For example, an individual tone sounded in the high range of a particular instrument may consistently be perceived as consonant, yet another individual tone sounded in that instrument's low range may ordinarily be perceived as dissonant. Or, with any given instrument, two tones played at the interval of a *3rd* may sound pleasant in one octave, yet they may sound unpleasant in another octave.

For the most part, the aforementioned effects are realized because of harmonics, which is a subject that is far from elementary, one which involves a huge number of variables. As it is not within the scope of this book to provide an elaboration on harmonics, you may wish to further investigate the harmonic series to acquire a better understanding of tone creation, the effect of instrument design on tone, and the effect of tone on tone.

*Listener*- Essentially, the listener decides what sounds "nice" and what doesn't. What may seem consonant to one person may seem dissonant to another. Furthermore, what may seem pleasant or soothing to any given listener on one day may seem irritating or aggravating the next day. The condition or mood of the listener at the time of hearing greatly affects his or her perception of the material that the composer/performer presents. At any given time, simple tone combinations can seem consonant or dissonant, or even an entire work as a whole can seem consonant or dissonant. The listener has the final say in these matters.

Inevitably, some readers might become concerned that the student who adopts the Scale Phrase System and System 2000 might be inclined to overlook traditional theory, namely the fundamentals of harmony. We believe, however, that each human being has the built-in devices that are needed for carrying out harmonic analysis; they're called "ears." Regarding the scales or the scale/chord combinations that you choose, you can be reasonably sure that if it doesn't work, you will find out soon enough. Your ears will let you know quickly what works and what doesn't work.

No matter which scale–chord combination you are working with, dealing with perceived dissonance is not a problem. You may either remove the offending tone, or use that tone as a passing tone instead of a chord tone. Ultimately, how you use tones in your compositions is entirely up to you. For music to be enjoyable for you, it must sound the way *you* want it to sound. There are no laws against using certain scales with certain chords. Be an artist. If you're an artist, you control the paint brush; it doesn't control you.

We offer the above list simply as a guideline and as an aid in helping you become familiar with the effect of scale–chord combinations. These combinations are not etched in stone, and there are many more potentially pleasing and workable combinations that are not listed here. Yes, some scales are odd, some chords are odd, and some combinations of scales and chords are odd; however, if *you* like them, then they're not so odd, are they?

# Chapter 16

# TONE LINING

In addition to having developed the three systems that are featured in this book, we have evaluated the terminology used in denoting orchestral lines of tones. We believe that some of the traditional terminology still being used in orchestration texts is inaccurate, specifically regarding what is customarily referred to as "doubling" of tone lines. In actuality, lines of tones that are traditionally labeled as having been doubled, such as lines "doubled in unison" or lines "doubled in octaves," are, in most cases, lines that are not literally doubled. Let's examine the common practice of writing lines of tones, a practice that we have chosen to refer to as *tone lining*.

When we compose a piece of music, we can write a line of tones to be used as a prominent (melodic) line, and we can write lines of tones to be used as subordinate (harmonic) lines. If we need a distinct line of tones to convey the prominent line, or main melody, we can employ *solo lining*. We can write a line of tones to be played by one instrument alone—without any tonal support whatsoever; this would be "solo" writing in the truest sense. Or, we could write a prominent line of tones for one instrument, and that instrument would be harmonically, yet subordinately, supported by one or more instruments. To the average listener hearing the average piece of music, solo lining would ordinarily automatically be perceived; the prominent line would stand out in such a fashion that the listener would ordinarily take the aural cue with little or no effort.

If we wish to make any given line "thicker" or "heavier," we can employ *unison lining*; for example, Flute 1 and Flute 2 can play the same line. This is what has been traditionally referred to as "unison duplication" or "unison doubling." In this particular example, true duplication or doubling of the given line of tones would be effected; that is, Flute 1 duplicates the line played by Flute 2, and, as there are only two instruments involved, the line can be said to have been literally "doubled." In most cases, however, the traditional term "doubling" proves to be semantically inaccurate. If more than two like instruments are playing the same line, then you might have tripling, quadrupling, or any other multiplication of that particular line. In the case of a Violin 1 section, with each member creating the very same tone, you would not have literal "doubling"; you would have duplication in as many multiples as there are players in the Violin 1 section.

If we wish to make any given line thicker, or fuller, while also making it "richer in color," we can also employ unison lining using *unlike* instruments; for example, the flutes, oboes, and clarinets can play the very same line of tones. This, too, has been traditionally referred to as unison duplication or unison doubling. The performers, using unlike instruments, are reading and consequently playing the same written "note"; and they may indeed be respectively producing a given tone at the very same frequency; however, the "color" of the tone sounded on instrument A will not be the same as the color of the tone sounded on unlike instrument B. As unlike instruments produce tones of distinctly different qualities, unison doubling, in the truest sense, is not effected. Given the above, using the term *unison lining* would be less confusing for beginners, and it would suggest that particular orchestral technique more accurately.

If we wish to "open up" the vertical plane of sound, while simultaneously exploiting select harmonic partials, we can employ *octave lining*. Traditionally, the term used for this application of tone lines has been referred to as "octave duplication" or "octave doubling." Here, too, we run into the same problem that we run into with the so-called "unison doubling."

If, for example, the Violin 2 section played a soprano part with the tessitura falling in the C4-C5 octave, the Violin 1 section could play the line one octave higher, in the C5-C6 octave. The Violin 1 section, however, will literally neither duplicate nor double the tone line played by the Violin 2 section. Granted, a given player of the Violin 1 section would indeed be duplicating the tone of his or her own group member—and go well beyond truly "doubling" any given tone in the section's assigned line—but that player would neither be duplicating nor doubling the tone played by any of the members of the Violin 2 section. Given the above, using the term *octave lining* would be less confusing for beginners, and it would suggest that particular orchestral technique more accurately.

If we wish to support a given line by harmonically thickening that line, we can employ *parallel lining*; that is, we can write lines that are virtually parallel to our given line, yet those new lines would be at intervals that are neither at unison nor at any octave from that given line. The intervals commonly chosen for parallel lining are *thirds* and *sixths*. For example, the Cello section could play a line in the mid-to-upper C4-C5 octave; the Violin 1 section could play a line an interval of a *third* lower; and the Viola section (all or part) could play a line an interval of a *sixth* lower. The traditional term used for this method of tonal line support is "non-octave doubling." Granted, in the above example, there would be duplication: each member of a given section would obviously be duplicating tones, and, of course, in multiples determined by the number of players in that section. But between instrument groups, with one group sounding a totally different line of tones than another group, duplication or doubling (or any other multiple) is physically impossible. In fact, in the case of parallel lining, the term "non-octave doubling" is actually far more inaccurate than either the phrase "unison doubling" or "octave doubling" would be in its own respective application.

And finally, if we wanted one instrument or one group of instruments to play a line (ordinarily, the prominent line), and then, at some point, pass the line onto another instrument or group of instruments, we would employ alternating-instrument lining, or *alternating lining*. We can safely use the abridged term, *alternating lining*, because the "alternating instrument" quality, in most cases, would be recognized naturally. Tonal differentiation itself (e.g., color, weight, luminosity) will ordinarily reveal instrument change. The line passed from one group to the next could actually be the same exact line of tones, though ordinarily it won't be; in contemporary compositions, lines are ordinarily not hackneyed through repetition, such as they often were in the Classic period. And even if the line is passed from one instrument to another *like* instrument, the "alternating" quality will not be lost. Granted, modern composers are keenly aware of the "long line"; that is, they will ordinarily tie the last note played by one group into the first note played by the following group. Here again, however, tonal differentiations will almost always preserve the sense of alternation.

We can see, then, that true duplication or doubling of lines of tones is not nearly as common as one would be led to believe. All in all, the new terms—*solo lining*, *unison lining*, *octave lining*, *parallel lining*, and *alternating lining*—are semantically, musically, and logically superior to the traditional terms. Whether or not they will be embraced by contemporary composers remains to be seen.

"Naming is a necessity for order, but naming can not order all things. Naming often makes things impersonal, so we should know when naming should end."—*Tao Te Ching*, translation by John H. McDonald

# INDEX

**A**

Accidentals, 9, 77
Add-on chords, 79, 81, 84, 90
Aeolian mode, 12, 13, 41, 42, 54
Ahavoh Rabboh mode, 46
Altered Harmonic Scale, 46, 51
Altered Major Scale, 46, 51
Altered Minor Scale, 47, 51
Altered Minor 2 Scale, 47, 51
Alto clef, 16, 23
Augmented Diminished Scale, 43, 50
Augmented Minor Scale, 43, 50
Augmented Minor 2 Scale, 48
Augmented Scale, 37, 40, 49
Augmented 2 Scale, 43, 50

**B**

Ban Shiki Cho Scale, 58
Baritone clef, 15
Base chord, 66, 73
Bass clef, 15
Bass tone, 71
Bithynian mode, 44, 54
Blue notes, 57
Blues Scale, 57
Brace line, 20, 21
Bracket, 20, 21

**C**

Carian mode, 44, 54
C clef, 15, 16, 17
Chinese Scale, 59
Chord, 73
Chord tones, 73
Cilician mode, 45, 54
Clef, 9
Clef degree, 23, 26
Clef indicator, 17
Clef type, 22, 23
Common line, 20, 21
Compound intervals, 29

**D**

Diatonic, 41
Dominant, 10, 67
Dominant chord, 67, 68
Dorian mode, 11, 12, 13, 39, 54
Diminished Augmented Scale, 45, 50
Diminished (H) Scale, 56
Diminished (W) Scale, 56

**E**

Egyptian Scale, 58
Eight-tone scale, 7, 10, 49, 50, 51
Eleventh (11th) base chords, 86
Enharmonic, 7, 33, 55, 57
Enigmatic Scale, 53
Equal temperament, 8, 85

**F**

F clef, 15, 16, 17, 22, 23
Fifth (5th) base chords, 74

**G**

Galatian mode, 43, 54
G clef, 15, 16, 17, 22, 23
Glarean modes, 54

**H**

Half step, 8, 9, 28, 30, 31
Half Step Scale, 55
Harmonic Minor Scale, 42, 45
Harmonic Minor 2 Scale, 46, 51
Harmonic Overlap Scale, 57
Harmonic Scale, 45, 51
Harmonic Series, 68, 85, 92
Hira Joshi Scale, 59
Hon Kumoi Joshi Scale, 59
Hungarian Gypsy Scale, 47
Hungarian Major Scale, 53
Hungarian Minor Scale, 46

**I**

Interval, 8, 27, 28, 29, 30, 77
Ionian mode, 12, 13, 39, 54
Iwato Scale, 59

**K**

Key signatures, 13, 14
Key tone, 9, 10
Kumoi Scale, 59

**L**

Locrian mode, 12, 13, 44
Locrian M2 Scale, 44, 50, 93
Locrian Scale, 41, 49, 93
Lycian mode, 43
Lydian Augmented Scale, 43
Lydian Dominant Scale, 43
Lydian Minor Scale, 48
Lydian mode, 12, 13, 40

**M**

Major Augmented Scale, 48
Major Harmonic Scale, 45, 51
Major Locrian Scale, 48
Major Minor Scale, 40, 49
Major Minor 2 Scale, 44, 50
Major Scale, 37, 39, 49
Melodic Minor Scale, 42
Mezzo-soprano clef, 15
Minor Augmented Scale, 44, 50
Minor Harmonic Scale, 51
Minor Major Scale, 42, 50
Minor Minor 2 Scale, 49
Minor Scale, 39, 49
Minor Six-Tone Scale, 58
Minor 3 Scale, 41, 49
Minor 2 Augmented Scale, 41, 49
Minor 2 Harmonic Scale, 47
Minor 2 Major Scale, 47
Minor 2 Minor Scale, 43, 50
Minor 2 Scale, 39, 49
Mixolydian mode, 12, 13, 40, 54
Modality, 14
Mode, 11
Mode signatures, 14
Modified chords, 77,79,82, 88, 90
Modifier, 69, 70, 71
Mysian mode, 42

**N**

Natural Minor Scale, 42
Neapolitan Major Scale, 47
Neapolitan Minor Scale, 47
Ninth (9th) base chords, 75
Note, 7

**O**

Octave, 95
Octave identification, 15
Omission of 5ths, 84
Oriental Scale, 53

**P**

Pamphrylian mode, 43
Pentatonic Scale, 58
Phrygian mode, 12, 13, 39
Pitch, 7
Pitch indicator, 17, 22
Post-Glarean modes, 54

**Q**

Quality of intervals, 27

**R**

Relative minor, 14
Ritusen Scale, 58
Root tone, 66, 72

**S**

Scale, 9
Scale-chord combinations, 93
Scale construction, 37, 38
Scale degrees, 10
Scale phrase, 31, 32, 33, 34, 35, 61
Scale Phrase Ways, 62, 63
Schumann Resonance, 17
Seconds (2nds), 8, 29
Seventh (7th) base chords, 75
Simple intervals, 28
Six-Tone Scale, 58
Size indicators, 66, 68, 71
Slash, 71, 72
Soprano clef, 15
Staff degrees, 9, 27
Staff systems, 15, 16, 19
Stave, 9
Superposed 3rds, 74
System C clef, 17, 18, 19, 20, 22, 23, 24, 25
System identifiers, 20
System 2000, 65
System 2000 rules, 77, 78, 80, 81, 83
System 2000 symbol order, 71

**T**

Tenor clef, 15, 16
Thirteenth (13th) base chords, 86
Timbre, 95
Todi Scale, 53
Tonality, 14
Tone, 7, 8
Tone lining, 97
Tonic, 9, 10
Treble clef, 15
Type indicators, 66, 71

**U**

Unusual scale phrases, 36

**V**

Vertical order of 3rds, 76, 87

**W**

Whole step, 31
Whole Step Scale, 55

# NOTES

# NOTES

Made in the USA
Charleston, SC
27 May 2015